✦   THE SWEDISH SECRET   ✦

THE

Swedish Secret

*What the United States Can Learn
from Sweden's Story*

Earl Gustafson

SYREN BOOK COMPANY

MINNEAPOLIS

Most Syren Books are available at special quantity discounts for bulk purchases for sales promotions, premiums, fund-raising, and educational needs. For details, write

Syren Book Company
Special Sales Department
5120 Cedar Lake Road
Minneapolis, MN 55416

Published by
Syren Book Company
5120 Cedar Lake Road
Minneapolis, MN 55416

Printed in the United States of America on acid-free paper

ISBN 978-0-929636-60-3

LCCN 2006921013

Second printing

Cover design by Kyle G. Hunter
Book design by Wendy Holdman
Cartoon reproduced on page 129 © cartoonbank.com.
Used by permission.

To order additional copies of this book see the form
at the back of this book or go to www.itascabooks.com

This book is dedicated to my fourteen grandchildren:

Casarah	Junita
Cori	Katie
Emma	Lara
Erin	Marcus
Gabriella	Nicole
Jessica	Shantraya
José	Sophie

Contents

Part Two: Contrasting Sweden and the United States Today

Preface

I STARTED WRITING THIS BOOK for my own edification and for my fourteen grandchildren—a racially diverse group of young Americans who carry the blood of Swedes, Africans, Mexicans, Norwegians, Serbians, Egyptians, and Puerto Ricans. Obviously, our family gatherings offer visual proof of one of the striking differences between Sweden and the United States.

The initial idea of comparing Sweden and the United States came to me after I'd prepared a booklet of family history for a summer reunion. As a second-generation Swedish American whose grandparents emigrated to the United States in the 1880s and 1890s (the precise place and date of the birth of my grandmother on my father's side is unknown), I realized how little I knew about the history of both Sweden and the United States. As I started to read about both countries, I became more engaged and fascinated by their remarkable similarities and fundamental differences. That prompted my third trip to the country in 2003.

At one point, my writing coach, Virginia McCullough, asked: "Why are you writing this book? What is your passion?" Let me explain.

Since my youth, I've been curious about how life works for all humankind collectively. Not what we are taught in school so much, but how things *really* work for groups of people in organizations such as families, businesses, gangs, athletic teams, faith communities, political parties, society, and governments. Let me explain further by recounting a story I heard about Richard Nixon that resonates with me. When Nixon visited a new town or city while campaigning, he demanded that his aides or advance people find out who was in charge and how things *really* worked in that community. He never assumed that the mayor or council members were the key people. It seems that Richard Nixon and I have one belief in common. When it comes to understanding legislative bodies, businesses, athletic teams, countries, or any human organization, immediate judgments are often wrong. It requires time to dig deeper before you can figure out how things function.

As I grew up, my relationships within groups provided my education. First, of course, was family and then school pals and teammates. Later, at age sixteen, I worked summers as a Great Lakes seaman and in my dad's store, and I also learned about group dynamics as a high school and college quarterback. After enlisting in the Navy at seventeen and completing boot camp, I "pushed" a platoon of new recruits through training and learned even more about how groups work.

College was fun and not too demanding. Along with other veterans of World War II, I had the support of the GI Bill, which gave me two years of free education at Gustavus Adolphus College, a Swedish Lutheran school in southern Minnesota. I loved courses in sociology and philosophy and graduated with a degree in business and economics. My best academic experience was an assignment in philosophy class to write our own vision of a utopian country. (I now regret that I lost that paper long ago.) Let me quickly add that I don't consider either Sweden or the United States a utopia, but I continue my obsession to find out how each country works. In talking this over with my daughter, Kim, she reminded me that she gave me a test years ago that indicated personality type and I came out strongest as an "observer." I don't disagree with that conclusion, but only quibble if this label also connotes passivity, because I've been an active person all my life.

While a senior in college, I met my love and life companion, Donna, and two years later we were married. At the time I told her I was planning to get a law degree and later a master's degree in political science so that I could teach political science or economics in a small midwestern college. These weren't exactly false representations, but my plans changed after we had our first child and law practice started to look more attractive than an academic life. An even greater impact was the advice I was given by my professor and adviser in graduate school in 1952, Dr. Dayton McKean, a well-known political scientist whose specialty was American politics and who also was the dean of the University of Colorado Graduate School. He knew I had finished my first year of law school at the University of Minnesota and also knew about my tentative plans for a career similar to his. He told me in confidence and in all candor: "Don't do it. You have a love for and interest in politics and government, and you will have more fun in this realm as a lawyer and participant than as an academic." I took his advice and don't regret it. (Donna initially did regret it, but she has forgiven me and has been supportive over the fifty-five years of our partnership.)

Doctor McKean was right. I graduated from law school in 1954 and returned to my home town of Duluth, Minnesota, to practice law with a small general practice firm, gravitating into litigation and administrative (governmental) law. In 1962, a local state representative resigned, and I was recruited by the area Democratic and union establishment to run for the legislature.

I won the election and started learning firsthand about how things really work in politics and government. By this time I was thirty-three years old and we had five kids. (Later we adopted three more.) To this day I'm grateful for the support my wife and law partners provided. I won four elections and served four terms in the Minnesota legislature, three in the House (one as assistant minority leader), and one in the state Senate. My experiences during these years would be fodder for another book. It was fun—a roller coaster—and worth more than a master's or Ph.D. in political science anytime.

After eight years in the Minnesota legislature, I realized I was something of a square peg in a round hole. For a while it was fun being a minor celebrity. Duluth has three TV stations with a dearth of breaking news, so it was easy to get interviewed for the latest legislative "report" from St. Paul and build what I had learned in politics was all-important: "name recognition." But to me the satisfaction that came from being a legislator was minimal, and the time demands kept increasing and stretched me too thin. Although I was exhilarated when I passed legislation that befitted my constituents or when I won an election, I realized my life had become split into thirds: family, legislature, and law practice. Fortunately, up to that time the legislature met every other year, but unfortunately, special sessions were increasing. It was time to drop the legislative third of my life, and I decided not to run in 1972.

Since then, Donna and I have raised eight different and interesting children. I served as a state tax court judge for seventeen years, and she ran a bed-and-breakfast in our big house in St. Paul for ten years. We met interesting guests from all over the country, including the late Paul Wellstone, who regularly stayed with us during his first run for the United States Senate. He and Sheila Wellstone became our friends and remain our inspirations. We share completely their conviction that the United States should work for everyone, and the best vehicle, to borrow Paul's phrase, is through the democratic wing of the Democratic Party and (my phrase) sensible Republicans.

So why have I written this book?

It started as a personal quest to compare and contrast Swedish and American history. It has now become something more than that. Through my reading, I relived how I personally witnessed the magnificent achievements our country made when it was unified and acting collectively. As a child, I have memories of how the nation recovered from a painful economic depression that affected everyone. My dad almost lost his small business during that time, and there was talk in our family about selling our house. But the country recovered through collective public action.

Next, as our country and our allies fought—and won—World War II, everyone was mobilized to share the load and the pain. Women went to work in the shipyards in our town, and as a teenager I helped the war effort when I sailed on a Great Lakes boat that hauled iron ore from Duluth and Superior to the steel mills in Chicago and Erie, Pennsylvania. After the war, our country willingly helped to rebuild a devastated Europe and Japan. The nation again made a huge investment after the war with the GI Bill, which allowed millions of veterans to attend college. Later, in the 1950s, an interstate highway system was built that binds the nation together economically and socially. All this was done successfully through intelligent public spending. It must be evident why most of my generation does not consider the government the enemy. After all, in a democracy we are the government.

What concerns me today is how the two countries have diverged so significantly over the past twenty-five years. The dominant ethos of America's conservative right has become the supreme importance of individual wealth accumulation and achievement. Any governmental regulation or taxation that might cause some personal restraint is considered harmful to the republic. Big-government social programs are thought to be wasteful. In contrast, the Swedish ethos (shared by most Western nations) is to pursue the common good and accept as appropriate the government's role in providing a universal safety net, quality education, and health care for all its citizens.

I never expect the United States to suddenly become another Sweden, but if we are able to make comparisons free of preconceived stereotypes, much can be learned. So, the impetus for this book comes from my love of family and country and a growing concern, based on my personal experience and study, of the destructive path the country has been taking.

The book itself traces the early and recent history of these two significant Western industrial democracies and their divergence after World War II. In the final chapters, I make some current comparisons between the countries in areas such as health care, foreign affairs, economic health, and taxation and conclude with a chapter on why Sweden works for everybody.

For helping me keep my eye on the ball, I thank my wife, Donna; my writing coach, Virginia McCullough; my friend Nancy Helin; my editor, Mary Byers; and my publisher, Maria Manske.

Introduction

CLOSE YOUR EYES AND IMAGINE a country where there is practically no homelessness; there has been no war for two hundred years; there is quality health care for all; there is excellent free public education through the college level; all in need are cared for; wages are high and there is low unemployment; voter participation is high without TV election ads; the economy grows without creating extremes of wealth alongside poverty; and there is little national debt. You don't have to imagine this nation. It exists. It is Sweden today.

How did this happen when we in the United States have been told that we can't have a dynamic national economy and generous social expenditures at the same time? Constrasting the recent history of the United States and Sweden may help us to find an answer.

The two countries were on a similar path until after World War II. It was in that period that the United States fought the Korean War, the Vietnam War, and the cold war, and gradually turned politically to the right, emerging as an economic and military superpower. At the same time, Sweden became economically prosperous but took a political left-hand turn, remaining fiercely neutral in foreign affairs and becoming one of the most democratic and egalitarian nations in the world. How did this split happen? Both have capitalistic economies and societies that protect free expression and religious choice. One is small, about the size and shape of California with a population of 9 million. The other is much larger—the third most populous country in the world—with 300 million people.

The smaller one, of course, is Sweden, a neighbor of Norway, Finland, and Denmark in Northern Europe. It has an ancient history going back to the Vikings and before. After many kings and their innumerable wars, it has evolved into a modern industrial democratic state with a literate citizenry that prizes excellence in all of their undertakings. Since abandoning military adventures, independence and neutrality have become its foreign policy. All studies show that Sweden is one of the world's most egalitarian nations—in terms of both gender equality and economic disparity between rich and poor.

What about the United States of America? At the end of the twentieth century and beginning of the twenty-first century, it has become the richest and most powerful nation in the world—and certainly one of the most diverse. Except for its indigenous natives, it has always been a country of immigrants. Some came willingly and some came in shackles. First came English settlers and then some Dutch and Swedes in the 1600s. They formed colonies along the eastern seaboard and later combined their thirteen colonies into a confederation that in the 1700s fought a war of independence against England and its monarchy. After the war, by written constitution, a federal republic was formed that was joined by all thirteen colonies. It was not yet a representative democracy because only men of property could vote and hold office, while women and slaves were denied any participation. But, since no true democracies existed at the time, Americans can rightfully claim that the United States was a representative republic and the first successful attempt by people of European heritage to form a democratic system free from any heredity nobility.

This new country of thirteen states, through immigration, purchase, and war, swiftly grew into a prosperous nation stretching "from sea to shining sea." The union was tested and solidified through a bloody civil war that permanently eliminated chattel slavery and the economic system on which it was based. In the words of Abraham Lincoln, it was becoming a nation "of the people, by the people, and for the people," which remains its goal today.

By 1900, the United States had recovered from the Civil War and had fought the Spanish-American War, its first significant imperial adventure that resulted in the acquisition of the Philippine Islands and Puerto Rico from Spain. President William McKinley was assassinated by an anarchist at Buffalo, New York, in 1901 at the beginning of his second term, and Theodore Roosevelt, his vice president, a vigorous, colorful New York politician, became a Republican president who promised to "speak softly and carry a big stick" in foreign affairs. At home he railed against the power and evils of big business trusts.

Sweden, in 1900 a much smaller country with only five million people, was also becoming industrialized. Cities like Stockholm and Göteborg grew as people moved from rural areas to urban centers. During this period, emigration provided the striking differences between the two countries. Sweden, a very poor country, had excess population. The United States was a growing, prosperous country, willing and able to accommodate new waves of immigrants. Many came from many different countries, including over one million from Sweden.

During the twentieth century, both countries grew more democratic and more industrialized. In Sweden, the political power of the king was virtually eliminated, but he remained accepted and honored as the symbolic head of state. Both countries were slow to allow universal suffrage for all women and men without property. Property qualifications for men were gradually eliminated, and women gained the right to vote in Sweden in 1918 and in the United States in 1920 with the enactment of the Nineteenth Amendment to the Constitution.

The two countries proceeded to develop economically on parallel tracks until after World War II. They started to diverge dramatically after 1950. This is when the full program of the ruling Social Democratic Party began and was systematically implemented and accepted by the Swedish people. It was commonly called "The Welfare State," or during the cold war "The Middle Way." It required higher taxes while providing so-called cradle-to-grave universal health care and social services.

In March 1987, the British magazine, the *Economist*, called Sweden "an economic paradox. It has the biggest public sector of any industrial economy, the highest taxes, the most generous welfare state, the narrowest wage differentials, and powerful trade unions. According to the prevailing wisdom, it ought to be suffering from an acute bout of 'eurosclerosis' with rigid labor markets and arthritic industry. Instead, Sweden today has many large and vigorous companies, and one of the lowest unemployment rates in Europe."

When Sweden suffered a recession a few years later and unemployment soared, the Social Democrats were voted out of power. The *Economist* prematurely announced, "The defeat of the Social Democrats has been described as the final nail in the coffin of the 'Swedish model,' once hailed as offering a third way between capitalism and communism." But the welfare state didn't roll over and die that easily. The Social Democrats were voted back into power in the national elections of 1994, 1998, and 2002.

Today both countries score high in economic growth. Compared with other industrial democratic countries, however, Sweden consistently is among the highest in social expenditures, voter turnout, equitable distribution of wealth, and support for foreign aid. The United States, on the other hand, is always among the lowest in these categories and has the highest rate of poverty.

Both countries have free market economies and proclaim the same goals of free speech, democracy, and justice for all. Yet, since 1950, they have traveled very different paths. How that happened and perhaps why that happened is the subject of this book.

PART ONE

The Story of Two Countries

CHAPTER I

Sweden Today:
Small, Rich, Egalitarian

Today, as individuals, Swedes seem like Americans. However, they know much more about us than we do about them, and most have at least one living relative in the United States. To an American, Swedes may seem to be different in some ways, but not all that different. We look at Swedes and see that they live a middle-class lifestyle, have a car and 1.7 children, and that both parents work outside the home. No matter how rich or poor, Americans like to say they are middle-class. Swedes will tell you the same thing, but they actually *are* mostly middle-class. Citizens of both countries complain about their taxes, but Swedes have more to complain about. The extremes between poverty and enormous wealth are not nearly as evident in Sweden as they are in the United States, where, in 2000, the richest *1 percent of American households owned 40 percent of all private wealth.*

Swedes adhere to an important principle that is expressed by a single word, *lagom,* which means "just enough." It comes from ancient Viking days, when people drank from a common bowl and had to be careful to leave enough for others. It remains a natural and accepted guide to personal and public life, and can be thought to essentially mean "moderation in all things." Just the opposite message from a zeitgeist that tells us: "There's never enough" or "the sky's the limit."

Another word loaded with special meaning in Swedish is *jäm-likhet* (equality). It dovetails with *lagom* (moderation) and is the governing principle ideologically proclaimed by the dominant Social Democratic Party and accepted by most Swedes. The Swedish concept has a more universal and far-reaching meaning than the equality we follow in the United States, where our Declaration of Independence says, "All men are created equal," which has been expanded over time to include both genders and all races. Our goal in the United States is not actual equality among people but rather equality of opportunity for all people. Sweden has the same goal of equal opportunity but has advanced further along this path, thereby achieving greater equality, in fact.

The Swedes I have met over the years usually look upon their American relatives as more affluent than themselves, and sometimes they may be correct. I don't know. But I do know that what they pay for health care and a good education is much less than American families must pay. Many Swedes travel and vacation in both winter and summer because five-week paid vacations are standard, and many have the discretionary money travel requires. I read in my Swedish-American weekly newspaper that there were over 20,000 Swedes vacationing in the Indian Ocean region, mainly in Thailand, when the tsunami struck the day after Christmas in 2004. Some 522 Swedes died in the disaster or are missing and presumed dead, causing national mourning and concern and prompting the prime minister as well as the king and queen to visit the disaster area.

Two myths about Sweden should immediately be discarded. First is that Sweden is a den of "free love." Based on my anecdotal unscientific information, this simply isn't true. What is true is that Swedish attitudes toward sex and nudity are traditionally more relaxed than in many other countries, and parents and children share more openness and frankness about birth control. Premarital sex is treated more as a health issue than a religious one. Predictably, Sweden is very far down on the global list of incidence of teenage pregnancies and sexually transmitted diseases.

A more serious myth harbored by many Americans is that Sweden is an all-controlling "socialist state" that stifles economic enterprise, in contrast to the United States, which is a country of "free enterprise" that encourages innovation and productivity. Nothing could be more untrue. Both countries are capitalistic, free market countries with a long history of scientific innovation and productivity. We had Benjamin Franklin and Sweden had Alfred Nobel! Before there was either a United States or a Sweden, the Vikings from the North traveled to what is now Poland, Russia, Turkey, and beyond as traders, or businessmen, as we would call them today.

In the twentieth century, Sweden industrialized rapidly, catching up with the United States and Western Europe. Swedish scientists and engineers emerged as some of the most brilliant in the world. Universal education and a high literacy rate were undoubtedly the key. Designers, too, worked to produce goods that were not only practical, but also good to look at, and industrialists drew on the country's heritage as a great trading nation in order to export their products.

Despite its small population, Sweden is one of the world's great industrial nations geared toward exports. Its exports consistently exceed its imports, unlike the United States, which continues to have a ballooning trade deficit and a twin fiscal deficit that puts our country's economy at risk. Sweden's chief trading partners are members of the European Union and the United States, in this order: Germany, the United Kingdom, the United States, Norway, and the Netherlands. There has been a recent shift from raw materials like lumber and iron ore to industrial products and electronic goods. But wood and paper products remain the country's second-largest export.

A new, dramatically designed bridge/tunnel across the Øresund, the sound between Sweden and Denmark, opened in 2000 and now easily links Sweden to all of Europe by auto, truck, and train. The last time I was in Sweden we flew into the Copenhagen, Denmark, airport and took a van across the Øresund by bridge/tunnel into Malmö, Sweden, in twenty minutes, the same amount of time it would have taken to drive into central Copenhagen.

Ninety percent of Sweden's companies are privately owned and include Ikea, the world's largest furniture retailer; Tetra Pak, the world's leader in carton packaging for liquids; the wireless telecommunications company Ericsson; the home appliance company Electrolux; and the vehicle manufacturers Volvo and Saab-Scandia. H&M, a modestly priced fashion clothing business, has also built a successful global network, and the wealthy Wallenberg family owns the country's largest bank and has interests in many other industries.

Like the United States, Sweden's government would have to be considered "friendly" to business, because corporations have a low tax rate (28 percent) to keep them competitive in a world economy. Individuals pay very high taxes, particularly sales taxes, but receive generous public services in return. The government in Sweden owns most of the railroads and, with Norway and Denmark, jointly owns Scandinavian Airlines Systems (SAS), which primarily runs international flights.

The basic rights of freedom of expression, political participation, and freedom of religion are guaranteed in the constitutional documents of both Sweden and the United States. In fact, Sweden goes further into the economic realm by guaranteeing that governmental power shall be exercised for the benefit of all individuals "to secure the *right* to work, shelter, and education." Most Americans know very little about Sweden's human rights guarantees. I was appalled when a twenty-year-old acquaintance, having learned that I was writing this book, asked me, "Isn't Sweden one of those countries that doesn't have free speech?"

Sweden's elections have high voter turnout with a one-house multiparty parliamentary system that encourages more consensus governance than we have in the United States, where "winner takes all" tends to prevail.

The role of religion is trickier. Although both countries maintain a "wall of separation" between church and state, the Christian religion remains dominant in both societies. The United States, through public prayer, the Pledge of Allegiance in schools, presidential rhetoric, patriotic song, and currency stamped "In God We Trust," clearly endorses religion in general, but not a specific religion. Today, like the United States, Sweden is a multi-faith country, with Christianity dominant in the culture.

On January 1, 2000, the Lutheran Church lost its official designation as the state church in Sweden, along with its duty to maintain the official records of births and deaths. Nevertheless, it remains both a civil and religious source of identity and attachment for Swedes. Ironically, they attend church with less regularity than Americans do, but they uniformly embrace its teachings of social justice. Unlike so much of Europe and the United States, the Roman Catholic Church is almost absent in Sweden. Consequently, its teachings regarding the clergy, birth control, abortion, and marriage have little impact on Swedish society and politics. However, Sweden's public policies on war, the death penalty, and social justice are identical to the teachings of recent Catholic popes.

The Social Democrats' vision of a collective society, common to other Nordic countries, grew largely out of a Protestant-Lutheran culture, in which care for the weak is the responsibility of society as a whole. As one of God's children, you are your "brother's keeper," and all people merit your concern. This belief has become a reality and has been given the Swedish name *folkhemmet,* or "home of the people." The *folkhemmet* goes further than many countries by collectively funding health care, education, child care, pensions, and elder care from cradle to grave. This works well only if the economy is sufficiently vibrant and people are willing to share the necessary tax load. With some occasional modifications and refinements, it has worked quite well in Sweden for the past fifty years.

Both Sweden and the United States, unlike most of Europe, have vast open spaces. Seventy percent of Sweden is covered by forests, and its cities are relatively small. Stockholm, the largest city, has a population of 685,000 people. There are no huge, densely populated urban areas similar to the northeastern United States from Boston to Washington, D.C., or southern California from Los Angeles to San Diego. This means that no Swede has to go far to be in untamed natural scenery and enjoy nature's gifts. There is an ancient "right of common access" that allows people to ignore "No Trespassing" signs and enter private or public land to hike, swim, or dock a boat—as long as they cause no harm nor invade someone's immediate privacy. So, while private property is respected, it's not considered as sacrosanct as it is in the United States.

In Sweden, love of nature and protecting the environment are universal concerns, almost like a "national religion." Most Swedes live in cities in the southern third of the country, but many maintain modest summer cottages in the woods or by a lake, while the more affluent may have an elegant home in the Stockholm archipelago. The landscape is nearly identical to northern Minnesota, Wisconsin, and Michigan, so it's no surprise that many Swedish immigrants settled in the upper Midwest during the great migration of the late 1800s and early 1900s.

The beautiful capital city of Stockholm is called the Venice of the North because it is built on fourteen islands on the rocky eastern shoreline opposite Finland and Latvia where Sweden's fresh-water lake, Lake Mälaren, meets the Baltic Sea. Bridges span the narrow bays and channels between the islands, and everywhere there are parks, squares, and airy green spaces. One-third of the city is water, while another third is open park and woodland. Elegant old stone buildings line the waterfront, where cruise ships are often docked. There is no cluster of tall skyscrapers, but there are old and modern office buildings for financial and governmental business, and of course, hotels, department stores, theaters, and the ubiquitous McDonald's. One of the most impressive and pleasant experiences is taking the subway. The cars are spacious and clean, and the stations are lined with art by seventy different commissioned Swedish artists and tie together the entire metropolitan area of one million people, most of whom live in apartment buildings outside the downtown.

A few words are in order about the prestigious Nobel Prizes endowed by the Swedish industrialist and inventor of dynamite, Alfred Nobel. Every year on December 10, Alfred Nobel's birthday, the Nobel Prizes are presented in Stockholm. During a glittering ceremony hosted by the king of Sweden, the prestigious prizes are awarded in physics, chemistry, physiology or medicine, literature, and economics. Separately, the Nobel Peace Prize is selected by Norway and awarded in Oslo to avoid any suggestion of Swedish influence. That prize remains the world's greatest award for a contribution to peace and reconciliation. Martin Luther King Jr. was awarded this prize in 1964, Bishop Desmond Tutu in 1984, and former president Jimmy Carter in 2002. These prizes continue to exemplify Sweden's and Norway's passion for excellence and for world peace.

About a hundred years ago, Sweden was losing people, mostly to the United States and Canada. That trend has changed, because by the 1940s and 1950s, Swedes stopped leaving in large numbers. There was always some migration back and forth between other

Baltic countries, but only in the past twenty years has Sweden become the recipient of large-scale immigration from the Mideast, the Balkans, and Africa. About 12 percent of today's residents were born outside of Sweden. Many come as asylum seekers or to reunite with other family members, so some unknown percentage may return to their homeland when conditions permit. As Americans have experienced for centuries, immigrants bring their own customs and religions with them and usually settle in larger cities. For example, in Stockholm there are already at least three mosques, and Malmö, the closest port to Europe, has become a multicultural city with more than a quarter of the population of foreign descent.

Sweden's long period of cultural insularity has come to an end, but not without problems. A friend of mine is an African American woman who lived in Stockholm for a number of years. Joyce told me that the Swedes seemed hospitable and well intentioned, but she saw the difficulty immigrant African women had when Swedish women insisted that the African husbands not accompany their wives to all-female "orientation" meetings about Swedish life. Official policy has moved from attempting to immerse immigrants in Swedish culture and become "good Swedes" to greater recognition of the uniqueness and value of different cultures. This shift has led to a commitment by the public schools to teach the children of immigrants their own language as well as Swedish.

The Sweden we know today has traveled far from its origins as a rigid class society with nobles at the top and peasant farm workers at the bottom. This journey wasn't completed until the last half of the twentieth century, when the country constructed one of the world's most egalitarian societies. Changes and modifications will continue, but Swedish democracy appears well equipped to peacefully resolve the inevitable political conflicts that arise.

CHAPTER 2

The United States Today: Big, Rich, Divided

B ABIES BORN IN THE UNITED STATES will grow up in the richest, most powerful nation on earth, with a military establishment unmatched by any other nation for the foreseeable future. It has become the world's sole superpower. At the same time, and perhaps understandably, the United States (not necessarily Americans individually) is mistrusted by people worldwide. In fact, as we've seen, it is so despised by some who feel their religion and culture are under attack that they are willing to take their own lives to harm or destroy their nemesis, the Great Satan, the United States of America.

In addition, the United States is not only a military superpower but is the wealthiest nation on the face of the earth by any measure, with an economy twice as large as that of its closest rival, Japan. The state of California alone has become the fifth-largest economy in the world, bigger than France and just behind Great Britain. America has the oldest continuing democracy with immigrants from many other lands.

The United States is larger in size than all of Europe and has majestic open spaces, splendid cities, and extended seacoasts on both the Pacific and Atlantic oceans. It is rich in abundant agriculture and natural resources of water, minerals, and forests. It also has petroleum reserves and production, something that many industrial nations like Sweden and Japan are completely without. Its elite colleges and universities are the finest in the world and have been attended by foreign students who have returned home and risen to leadership positions in their own countries.

How much does the United States spend on military expenditures? Now about 5 percent of its annual gross domestic product (GDP) and 20 percent of the federal annual budget. With the invasion of Iraq, its reconstruction, and continued occupation, military spending will continue to increase. The massive funding of military research and development will also continue to increase and leave all other countries behind. The fact that conventional wars, nation against nation, have become obsolete seems to have little effect on our military budget and allocations. Currently, political realities have made Congress afraid to cut the military budget. While other countries' military spending has been declining relative to their GDPs, the American military-industrial complex is always ongoing and planning for the "next" war.

After the 2000 elections, the Republican Party had full control of the national government and the direction it chose to take the country. All three branches of government—executive, legislative, and judicial—were firmly in Republican hands. The evolution of power from the more progressive Democrats to the more conservative Republicans was complete. There are independent freethinkers in both parties, of course, but the conservative movement in America had triumphed. It probably started with the Democratic Party's embrace of the civil rights movement in the 1960s. Lyndon Johnson, a president from Texas, accurately predicted this realignment when he signed the Voting Rights Act of 1965 that guaranteed African Americans the right to vote. At that time there was a Democratic (but conservative) "solid South." But today, after the 2004 elections, only five of the twenty-two senators from the eleven states of the old Confederacy are Democrats.

The country is almost evenly divided, with the Democrats stronger in the Northeast, Upper Midwest, and West Coast, and the Republicans dominant in the South, the Central Plains states, and the Western mountain regions. The big cities outside the South, such as New York, Chicago, Boston, Philadelphia, Los Angeles, and San Francisco, are heavily Democratic, while smaller cities and towns and rural areas are strongly Republican.

What gave Republicans effective electoral power are a number of conservative beliefs or fables that have been identified with the Republican Party and accepted as absolutes by many Americans. Several are simplistic and some downright false. Not all are unquestioned by all Republicans. But enough are accepted uncritically by enough "true believers" to carry a potent political impact in elections. Some of these beliefs are the following:

- Public spending should be reduced to keep government as small as possible.
- The American people are overtaxed.
- Federal deficits don't matter.
- Free market capitalism is always more efficient than government action.
- Religious beliefs "given by God" should become law.
- Reducing taxes on the wealthy benefits everyone.

Because these beliefs have so powerfully dominated political thinking in the United States, they deserve examination.

Public Spending Should Be Reduced to Keep Government as Small as Possible

The promise to seek a smaller government has been consistently broken by both Republican and Democratic administrations and

Congress. One fiction Washington has adopted is that public spending for the military and mandatory entitlements like Medicare, Medicaid, and Social Security pensions, plus interest on the national debt and homeland security, should not be counted when you reduce government. This leaves only "discretionary" programs like education, welfare and farm subsidies, and so forth, to bear the pain of creating "smaller government." This means that only about one-seventeenth of the federal budget can be reduced. When Bill Clinton and the Republicans combined to "end welfare as we know it" in the 1990s, and claimed that "the era of big government is over," they were way off the mark. Since 2001, when George W. Bush started cutting taxes for the wealthy and increased the amount of money we borrowed from foreign governments, public spending has also continued to increase, so much so that the federal debt limit has had to be raised by Congress three times to reach its present staggering level of $8.2 trillion and growing.

No matter what the political parties say, public spending for the military, entitlements, and everything else government does is bound to increase. The reality is that, given the world we live in and the demands of the American people for security and their aspirations for fair and equal treatment for all, neither party will be able (or should) deliver on a promise of smaller government. The only question is whether we will adopt a "pay as you go" plan through fair taxation and balanced budgets or continue borrowing and leaving it to our children and grandchildren to deal with.

The American People Are Overtaxed

This notion is completely false. The question to ask is: compared to what? It may be unfair to compare us to Sweden because that nation offers generous public services and a safety net that most countries do not approach. But it is only fair to compare the United States to other Western industrial nations. According to the Organisation for Economic Co-operation and Development, which tracks such information, the United States has very low taxes, some of the lowest. The average total taxes (federal, state, and local) for the United States are 31 percent of its GDP compared to the average of 46 percent for European Union countries.

Federal Deficits Don't Matter

This is a myth perpetuated by Vice President Dick Cheney when he told other Bush II administration officials that "Ronald Reagan proved that deficits don't matter." That was a half-truth because Ronald Reagan ran up huge deficits while cutting taxes, and in the short run, it didn't adversely affect his popularity. The deficits did, however, affect the popularity of his successor, George Herbert Walker Bush, who had to deal with a fiscal mess that forced him to act responsibly and, much to his political detriment, break his oft-repeated pledge: "Read my lips, no new taxes."

What Dick Cheney was talking about was how federal deficits affect presidents politically in the short run. What is far more important is how deficits that cause a mounting national debt can endanger the whole society.

Peter Peterson, a lifelong Republican and former secretary of commerce, recently wrote a book, titled *Running on Empty: How the Democratic and Republican Parties Are Bankrupting Our Future and What Americans Can Do about It*, in which he discusses Dietrich Bonhoeffer, a German theologian and martyr. While awaiting execution by the Nazis, Bonhoeffer wrote, "The ultimate test of a moral society is the kind of world it leaves to its children." In commenting on these words, Peterson writes, "most of us understand that one essential duty of any citizen is speaking up and taking action when we see a great wrong threatening our republic's future. What is now happening fiscally is a great wrong."

The United States is running some of the largest annual deficits and far and away the largest national debt in our history. Six years ago we had a budgetary surplus and made payment on the national debt. More tax cuts and the partial privatization of Social Security as recently proposed by President George W. Bush would only reduce revenue and increase our national debt. It is a very scary scenario. All reputable economists and foreign central bankers agree that we seem to be losing control of fiscal discipline, just like a person hooked on credit cards.

Free Market Capitalism Is Always More Efficient Than Government Action

This is one of those partial truths that has become an absolute truth for many Americans, particularly conservative businesspeople. It is true that free market capitalism can be an efficient and flexible economic system. At least that is the dominant thinking in both the United States and Sweden, and other Western democracies as well. There is also universal agreement that government has a legitimate role in keeping the system free and fair in order to protect business, the environment, the general public, and the system itself from abuse, exploitation, and corruption.

What is not true is that the delivery of all services to the general public should be done through private profit-making organizations because they are more efficient. Think of private firefighting companies that, of course, would respond only to paid-up subscribers. When talking about efficiency, look at the enormous cost of health care in the United States that involves public entities plus a myriad of private profit-making organizations and insurance companies, each with its own terms, expenses, and rules.

Nothing could be more inefficient. No wonder we spend twice as much on health care as European countries such as Sweden.

The truth is that all large organizations, private or governmental, are susceptible to inefficiencies. All are run by humans. Think of the military. I had a law partner a few years my senior who spent four years in the Army during World War II in England, North Africa, and Italy. He loved to tell entertaining "war stories" at lunch with a fellow war veteran and myself. One of Jim's favorite pronouncements was, "The only reason we beat Germany was because they had an army, too."

Religious Beliefs "Given by God" Should Become Law

Despite the claim that there is a firm separation between church and state, certain religious teachings have such a strong political impact that some elections for federal offices can turn on these issues. Two examples that deal with private conduct are abortion and homosexuality. The goal of the politically active religious groups that oppose all abortions and homosexual marriages is to have their positions enshrined in law and applied to all citizens. In the case of homosexual marriage, some groups even advocate a constitutional amendment. Motivated by such religious certainty, they contend that candidates who do not agree with them have the wrong moral values and should be defeated regardless of their positions on other issues.

Actually, most Americans are not that certain about banning abortions under all circumstances and feel that committed homosexual couples should have legal rights similar to those of married couples.

Polls show that most people believe that a woman should be allowed to make the ultimate choice whether to have an abortion, in consultation with the father, and others, such as her parents, her doctor, and her religious adviser. Most disapprove of abortions as a method of birth control but think there should be exceptions in special circumstances such as incest, rape, and to save the life of the mother. Based on personal experience, after winning four elections to the state legislature as a pro-choice candidate, I found that most voters are not tied to a single issue, are independent and open-minded, and base their vote on many considerations, along with their personal evaluation of the candidate. This I learned early in my political career.

In my first campaign as a young candidate, I was invited to a closed meeting with a group of Catholic nuns who taught at a small college in my district. I was asked many questions and they gave me their views as well. I told them how my wife and I personally opposed abortion but that I also opposed criminalizing a woman's choice and would vote accordingly. After the meeting, their spokesperson called to say that after discussion they had reached a consensus: they agreed with me on most issues, so they would vote for me, despite my position on abortion.

Reducing Taxes on the Wealthy Benefits Everyone

The theory is that everyone benefits from growth in the economy. According to this thinking, rich people are creative and use their money to make more money and in the process create more businesses that, in turn, create new jobs. Therefore, it follows that if you reduce income taxes on the wealthy and on their already accumulated assets, everyone, even poor people, benefit. This is what critics call "trickle down" economics or "feeding the sparrows by feeding the horses." However, in reality, rich people who get more money when their taxes are reduced don't automatically spend their money creating new jobs. Most just increase their wealth through investments while they live off interest and dividends. Money is now invested globally, wherever there is the greatest return, so there is no guarantee that the money they receive from tax cuts will increase job growth in the United States.

As taxes on high incomes have been reduced, the gap between the wealthy and low-income individuals has increased. The $1.3 trillion tax cut of 2001 was a gift for people earning over $500,000 a year, who got 40 percent of its benefit. The tax cut of 2003 was even better for very high income people. Those with a net income of about $1 million got an average tax cut of $90,000 a year. For the typical middle-income family, taxes dropped just $217, and many low-income families, who are still subject to payroll taxes, got nothing. Census Bureau figures clearly show that a rising share of national income goes to the top 20 percent of families and that the 13,000 richest families have almost as much income as the 20,000,000 poorest families. The claim that reducing taxes on the wealthy benefits everyone has been proven to be a fairy tale.

To describe any realistic picture of the United States today, with its fifty different states, shaped by different waves of immigrants with diverse histories, is a hazardous undertaking. The best I can do is mention some of its paradoxes and divisions. One obvious division is the political one. The past two presidential elections, 2000 and 2004, were almost evenly split between Republicans and Democrats.

Too much analysis of this electoral division can be unproductive for three reasons. First, the presidential candidate himself and how he presents himself may affect a person's vote aside from any issues of public importance. Second, so-called wedge issues represent beliefs about private conduct like abortion and gay marriage rather than expressions about public policy like the national debt and Social Security. Third, the two consequential political parties include many differing groups within their big tents. It is wrong to consider them each as a solid unified force. As Will Rogers said, "I don't belong to any organized political party. I'm a Democrat." This is also true of the Republicans, who are probably more ideologically unified than Democrats. The congressional election of 2006 demonstrated the power of independent swing voters.

Some of the ideas Americans universally seem to agree on were best articulated by Abraham Lincoln, who asked for "liberty and justice for all" and for "government of the people, by the people, and for the people." These are enduring public moral values that should guide us as a country.

One of the great paradoxes in the United States is its unwillingness to even seriously address the issue of poverty. Fifteen to 20 percent of Americans live in poverty. There is a proclaimed recognition by the religious and political establishment that poverty in our rich country is a moral issue. Yet it continues to grow. My wife and I attended the annual dinner meeting of the local Council of Churches and we were given buttons to wear that said, "Overcoming Poverty *is* a Religious Issue!" In his inaugural address in 2001, President George W. Bush put it accurately when he stated, "In the quiet of American conscience, we know that deep, persistent poverty is unworthy of our nation's promise." Nevertheless, the two presidential candidates in 2004 spoke little about increased poverty, homelessness, and the plight of the working poor. It was all about the war in Iraq, terrorism, and the plight of the middle class, with some "wedge" issues about personal conduct thrown in.

America is largely a "Christian" country with high church attendance. Over half of all families say grace before shared meals. But the spiritual teachings of Jesus—love for neighbor, nonviolence, forgiveness, living simply and with humility—are largely ignored. In practice, America is a consumption society, and its government puts a premium on unrestrained private growth. The rich and powerful are rewarded and celebrated, and the poor and vulnerable are marginalized. A 2006 study by the Economic Policy Institute finds that the nation's income inequality gap is widening.

America today projects several different visions. It's a symbol of welcome, opportunity, progress, and success, but it's also a symbol of arrogance, intolerance, injustice, and inequality. The question follows: How can we maintain a strong military and a muscular foreign policy, and provide universal education and a healthy social safety net, if we continue to push for low taxes and a smaller government? How can we celebrate individual liberty and religious freedom if we pass laws against personal conduct based principally on religious beliefs? These are some of the paradoxes that divide the country and will continue to do so for years to come.

CHAPTER 3

Two Countries Long Ago

Unlike sweden, the United States formed itself in a new geographic place with people who had come from elsewhere. The native indigenous people were pushed aside. It evolved first as a collection of separate European colonies that later joined together and then became independent from its ruling mother country, England. Sweden, on the other hand, has a much older history and identity as a land that slowly became a national democracy by steadily eliminating the power and privileges of its nobles and monarchy. It retains its ancient sense of place in its Nordic peninsula in the Baltic region of Northern Europe.

After Columbus discovered the Caribbean islands on behalf of the Spanish Crown in 1492, no Spanish colonies were established that evolved similar to the United States. Spain, through various explorers, made many journeys into the mainland of North America after it had conquered and plundered Mexico and much of South America and the Caribbean islands. It planted its first North American settlement of St. Augustine in Florida in 1565. By that time it led the other major European powers, France and Holland, in exploring and exploiting the New World, with England lagging far behind.

The year 1588 was the turning point. England's surprising defeat of the powerful Spanish Armada marked the crest and eventual decline of Spain's power. No longer could the English, Dutch, or French colonization of North America be prevented. The English

Crown had already laid claim to the eastern seaboard through the voyage of John Cabot, which was commissioned in 1497 by King Henry VII. However, neither Henry VII nor Henry VIII did anything to develop the land claimed. Henry VIII's second daughter became Queen Elizabeth I in 1558, and she and her successor, King James I, transformed that claim into reality. The English Crown gave charters with grants of land to develop colonies to companies or individuals.

The new colonies were settled overwhelmingly by English immigrants, who brought with them a history of limited selfgovernment. The next largest group of colonists were Dutch, who bought land from the Indians and started a settlement called New Amsterdam, now New York City.

The original thirteen colonies that eventually banded together to become the United States were referred to as the New England Colonies, the Middle Colonies, and the Southern Colonies. The New England Colonies were developed under a charter given by King James I of England in 1606 to a group in England known as the Plymouth Company.

First came the Pilgrims on the *Mayflower* to Plymouth in the New England area in December of 1620.

Next, the Puritans arrived in larger numbers seeking religious freedom from the Church of England. During the summer of 1630, nearly a thousand people arrived in seventeen ships. Unlike the Pilgrims, who were poor and ill equipped, these new settlers came well provided with food, clothing, and necessary equipment. They built villages along the coast, including Shawmut, later called Boston. By 1640, more than 20,000 English settlers were living in the Massachusetts Bay Colony. New colonies of Rhode Island, Connecticut, New Hampshire, and Maine were subsequently established. Although all were independent of one another, they developed along similar self-government lines.

By the 1750s, thriving towns and cities had been built in New England around all usable harbors. Boston alone had a population of about 15,000.

Moving inland, many small villages appeared, usually started by friends and neighbors who belonged to the same church. Town plans included a central "common" surrounded by homes with farmlands in back. Typically there was a piece of land set aside for the church and town hall. The settlers adopted universal military training and organized militias, which were groups of citizens trained for military service but not on active duty except for times of emergency. This idea of a voluntary militia grew into the present-day mythology that all Americans have a constitutional right to carry concealed handguns and military rifles.

In 1619, the first Africans arrived, not as slaves but as indentured servants able to work off their debts and free to own land, a situation similar to indentured whites. This soon changed. By the 1640s, Africans were brought to Virginia as chattel slaves. The large plantations, whether growing tobacco or rice, required large numbers of workers. With plenty of land available to them on the frontier, free men would not work for low wages on the plantations. The planters began to rely more and more upon slave labor, which soon became the distinguishing characteristic of the Southern Colonies. Few people from the other colonies objected to slavery, but only the plantation South evolved into a "slave economy" rather than "an economy with slaves," which existed elsewhere.

Before the War of Independence, about one-sixth of the entire colonial population were slaves. In contrast, two-thirds of the inhabitants of South Carolina were slaves. Along the southern seaboard, slave labor clearly sustained the wealth and power of the white masters.

By 1700, England had successfully colonized the eastern seaboard of the future United States, with the exception of Florida.

Much to Britain's surprise, within a hundred years, these separate colonies somehow united, successfully fought a war of independence, and created a new "democratic" nation that eventually grew into the most powerful nation in modern history.

An estimated 750,000 people crossed the Atlantic Ocean between 1600 and 1770. A desire to escape the constant wars and upheavals in Europe was one reason they came. For some, it was a determination to avoid the possibility of being snatched into the armies of kings and princes embroiled in wars. For most, the desire to find work and make a better life for themselves and their families provided the primary motivation. Many were eager to escape religious persecution and be free from church and government domination. While most stayed in Europe and endured, those who broke away and came to the New World brought a spirit of energy, enterprise, daring, or aspiration that has remained throughout American history. The colonists did not remain docile subjects. They developed a new culture that increasingly separated them from their European roots of monarchy and inherited wealth and aristocracy.

On the Atlantic coastal plain in central North America, there were no large populations of people to conquer and rule for the benefit of a European Crown. What was available was a great deal of wild land for conversion to agriculture. The British wanted a large population of Europeans to quickly transform the forests into farms and permanent settlements to provide a market for English manufactured goods. Consequently, no restrictions on the number, religious affiliation, or nationality of immigrants were demanded by the English kings. Europeans of any nationality and religion could immigrate to these colonies if they were willing to take an oath of allegiance to the English king.

The individualistic behaviors and beliefs regarding social relations, worship, and political rights that developed in America were contrary to England's imperial interests. Yet, to a great extent, the permissive policies of colonial immigration and government adopted by the English Crown prompted these behaviors.

The reasons behind England's colonial policies had nothing to do with a more enlightened imperialism. England was racked by political strife and civil turmoil during most of the eighteenth century, when the colonies were founded. These troubles at home diverted the Crown's attention, allowing the colonists more leeway in governing themselves. In short, they were allowed a great degree of self-responsibility. In addition, the English kings made the colonists pay the cost of colonial administration, including the salaries of the governors appointed by the Crown. To pay these expenses they were allowed to elect an assembly in each colony to set the needed taxes. The colonial assemblies were elected by a much broader base of voters than elected the House of Commons in England and, of course, they had no House of Lords.

The open immigration policy set Americans on a different path of cultural development. No European country had ever had a self-selected population for its colonies in the New World. Land became owned by a larger portion of the population than had ever been true in England or any other European country, including Sweden. This general ownership of land proved fatal to the idea that colonies should remain subordinate to the interest of the monarchy that authorized them.

Until the British invaded Canada and drove out the French in 1760, no English troops had ever been stationed in their American possessions. Before that, the English Crown required the colonies to pay for their own defense in money and manpower. The taxes England tried to impose on these colonists in the 1760s were intended to make them pay for part of the cost of the French and Indian War of 1754–1763, for which Americans had provided some troops (including young George Washington).

By and large the Americans had already become independent of England by the 1760s or even before, but they didn't fully realize it. They were no longer Englishmen living in America, a fact that Thomas Paine saw clearly. In 1776 he published his famous essay, "Common Sense," in which he told Americans that they had no further need to defer to England's aristocratic culture, and should no longer be subservient to a government dominated by titled lords and a king. His writing was instantly popular because it confirmed the belief among Americans that the people are sovereign. The conditions of life in America during the previous century had already created that belief.

The colonists were able to build a strong agricultural economy. At the end of the colonial age at least nine-tenths of the white people lived on the land and produced for themselves what was necessary for a good, if often simple, living. A few thousand large landowners grew rich on tenant and slave labor and lived luxuriously. But most white people owned small farms and worked with their own hands in the fields, farmhouses, and forests. Others were shop owners. Life was hard, no doubt, but their self-supporting economy and their spirit of independence made the society different from Europe.

In England itself, the rapid growth of the mercantile class was weakening the hold of the old landed gentry and clergy on English government. In the colonies, where land was abundant, no class could monopolize all of it, and nowhere were the class lines absolutely rigid.

As England continued to extend its normal taxation and control over the colonies as subjects of the Crown, the colonists increased their resistance because they believed they were no longer Englishmen, but had become Americans who had established a new and separate identity. The inevitable next step would be some type of unification of the thirteen colonies for collective opposition.

That step was the First Continental Congress, formed in the 1770s. Meanwhile, in the 1770s, Sweden remained a hereditary monarchy with a weak parliament (Rickstag) dominated by nobles. Its evolution into a democracy would have to wait a hundred years.

Long before any Europeans reached North America, some of the inhabitants of Scandinavia (now Norway, Sweden, and Denmark) ventured south to set up colonies and began raiding other areas. They became known as the Vikings, a name derived from an Old English word meaning "pirate." Today, however, the word is often used to describe any Scandinavian person who lived during the years 800 to 1100—or more likely, a Minnesota football player.

The Danish and Norwegian Vikings went south and westward, concentrating on Western Europe and England. The Swedish Vikings went south and eastward into Russia and even as far as Jerusalem, Baghdad, and the Caspian Sea.

The Danish and Norwegian Vikings tended to conquer and colonize, while the Swedish Vikings more frequently entered into trade and did not seek to colonize. Only strong and relatively young men went on raids to other lands. Women, children, and older people stayed home and tended the farms that were the backbone of Viking society. A written language, trade centers, and established democratic forms of government were developed. In many respects, Viking society was tribal in that tight-knit groups worked together for the survival of everyone. The majority of people were freemen who usually owned land and were known as jarls. As more people lived closer together they formed villages. The person with the most land, hence the richest, became the head of the tribe. Sometimes a jarl became so powerful and rich that he became king in his own district.

A Viking woman's position in society was based on her husband's possessions, and women ran the farms while the men were away raiding and trading. Women could conduct business on behalf of their husbands, shaking hands to seal the bargain—just like a man would do. They possessed the household keys, a symbol of control. A woman had the right to divorce her husband if he kept the household keys from her or if he mistreated her.

Most marriages were arranged by parents, but many parents allowed their daughters to refuse the match. Married women owned their own property and shared equally in any property acquired during their marriage, and if they divorced, the woman would then take her property and return to her parents. Either party could divorce the other and were free to remarry.

The Vikings had great respect for the law, and nearly all members of society participated in the democratic process. Each local community had an assembly called a *thing* that controlled law and order. Each *thing* had its own set of laws and settled disputes between residents.

Most Vikings respected the laws and decisions declared by the *thing* because they preserved unity and harmony within the community. Anyone who did not accept the decision of the assembly became an outlaw and had to give up all of his or her land and possessions. They usually also had to flee the community because they had no legal protection and could be killed, without punishment to the killer. Throughout Viking society, the good of the whole community was of greatest importance.

Throughout the British Isles, Ireland, and the Baltic region, cities established by the Vikings are still flourishing. For example, the Vikings founded the city of Dublin, Ireland, in the year 850. The Viking Age ended about 1100, centuries before the so-called discovery of America by Columbus in 1492, which was actually discovered in 1003 by Leif Eriksson, a Norwegian Viking who sailed west from Greenland to reach land that was the eastern coast of present-day Canada.

The Viking influence remains in modern Sweden. Their permanent legacy is a democratic form of government and a strong commitment to collective welfare.

After the Viking Age ended, Sweden began establishing its identity through wars between nobles and warlords in the Baltic area, but subsistence farming was the principal occupation of people. Most tangible wealth was the land, which was owned by the Crown, the church (until the Reformation), the nobility, and freehold farmers. Great differences existed in wealth and status. Monarchs tended to amass large landholdings, and as a national state developed, the theoretical claim also developed that the king was the state and therefore originally "owned" all the land. Nobles with private armies (today we might call them warlords) made their forces available to the king who, in return, gave land that was tax exempt or "privileged." By the time the Reformation began in 1520, less than 10 percent of the land was owned by the Crown, approximately 50 percent by farmers, approximately 20 percent by the Roman Catholic Church, and approximately 20 percent by the nobility.

At one time in the 1400s and early 1500s, Sweden was linked with Denmark in what called the Kalmar Union. There was much discontent in Sweden about this arrangement, which was headed by the Danish king, and many plots developed among Swedish nobles to make Sweden independent.

In 1520, the Danish king, Christian II, invaded Sweden and had himself crowned king. What happened next was truly horrific. Thinking he would suppress any further attempts to separate Sweden from Danish domination, he had over eighty of Sweden's leading nobles invited to a banquet and then had them beheaded in what has come to be known as the Stockholm Bloodbath. This heinous action unleashed a new revolt led by a young nobleman, Gustav Eriksson Vasa, a son of one of the executed nobles, who led a campaign of commoners and nobles, driving the Danes from the country. In the process, Gustav Vasa got himself elected king in 1523, and then went on to found a hereditary dynasty that lasted for more than two hundred years.

According to legend, the peasants of Dalarna in western Sweden, near the border with Norway, traveled on skis a long distance to join Gustav Vasa and help him chase the Danish king out of the country. The event is celebrated today in the annual Vasaloppet, a ski race that has thousands of participants.

Gustav Vasa I proved to be one of Sweden's most significant monarchs and is considered to be the father of the early modern Swedish state, although some historians also say he was one of its most tyrannical kings. It is well known that he laid the foundations of many institutions, including a national army and navy.

By Gustav Vasa's time the Roman Catholic Church had spread Christianity north to Sweden, and he saw an opportunity to eliminate the powers of the church and increase state finances by supporting Martin Luther's Reformation that was sweeping Europe. He severed ties with the Roman Catholic Church, confiscated all church property, with the approval of parliament, and replaced it with the Lutheran Church of Sweden, whose clergy came under state control. Separation of church and state was unheard of.

Another strong king later in the Vasa dynasty was Gustav Adolph, or Gustavus Adolphus, who reigned from 1611 to 1632. He was a brilliant soldier who earned the nickname "The Lion of the North." He led the country into European wars and won battles against Denmark, Russia, and Poland. Present-day Finland, Estonia, Latvia, and regions of Germany were all parts of Sweden during this time, but the defense of these borders became increasingly difficult and costly. In 1630, Gustavus Adolphus intervened on the side of the Germany Protestant princes who were fighting the Holy Roman Emperor in Vienna. Leading an army south into

Central Europe, he was killed in battle in 1632, but he remains one of Sweden's historical military heroes.

The next to last of the Vasa kings was Gustav III, who came to the throne around the time of the American Revolution in 1771 and reigned until 1792. He founded the Swedish Academy for Literature, Music, Art, and History as well as the Royal Opera House and the Royal Dramatic Theater in Stockholm. He also granted freedom of worship. Thanks to the Vasa dynasty, Sweden was left with a rich artistic and cultural tradition as well as Lutheranism as the national religion.

As Gustav III's popularity and influence increased, so did the discontent of the Swedish aristocracy, who saw a resulting loss of their own power. They plotted against him and he was assassinated in 1792 during a masked ball. Giuseppe Verdi later composed an opera about this event.

Sweden's days as the leading power in the Baltic were over. The cost of those many wars was enormous, and eventually the willingness to bear them evaporated.

The history of an overseas empire was much shorter. The Swedish African Company was a private venture with government participation that established the beginnings of an independent settlement in 1638 along the Delaware River in America. It had a small number of settlers and little financial success. In 1655, the Dutch annexed the colony as part of New Netherlands. Eight years later the English, in turn, took over all the Dutch territories in North America. Interestingly, many of the Swedish colonists chose to stay, and they and their descendants helped shape American colonial history.

By the 1770s, when the Americans started to form their first Continental government, Sweden had strong social, economic, and governmental structures already taking hold. It was not yet a broad-based democracy, but it was moving in that direction.

CHAPTER 4

The United States: Creating a Democracy

T HE MIDDLE OF THE 1700S saw intermittent wars and constant rivalry between Britain and France. This extended to north America, where France claimed the land north (Canada) and west to the Mississippi River. The strife culminated in the French and Indian War in which Britain ultimately smashed French power south of Canada and claimed all the land east of the mississippi River, except the city of New Orleans. British redcoats and American colonists, including young George Washington, fought together against the French. The British Empire continued to grow around the world, including India, but was soon to lose its American colonies.

Britain was heavily in debt because of these wars and expected the colonists to help pay some of the costs, especially for their own defense. The colonies opposed any request to assume Britain's war debts, and colonial legislatures passed resolutions asserting that they alone had the right to levy taxes.

The resistance to British taxation and limitations on trade centered on Boston in the Massachusetts colony and culminated in crowds taunting and throwing rocks at British soldiers who attempted to keep order. On March 5, 1770, such a confrontation got out of hand and someone gave an order to fire. Three civilians were killed and two others mortally wounded. The city went wild with anger. A "massacre" the people called it, and they demanded that the British withdraw all troops from the city. Hostilities cooled temporarily when some of the more onerous laws were repealed by the English Parliament, but a small import duty on tea was retained.

In 1773 Parliament passed the Tea Act in an effort to help the British East India company, headquartered in England. The law removed the requirement that the company sell tea only to English merchants and permitted sales directly to the colonists, thus lowering the cost and saving money for the company, which was in financial trouble. What appeared to be a win-win solution had one problem: the law retained the small import duty, and now colonists were opposed to any and all taxes imposed by Parliament.

In 1773, colonists disguised as Indians boarded ships in Boston Harbor and heaved their cargoes of tea into the water. The Boston Tea Party, as it was called, brought a quick response from the English Parliament, which passed four measures designed to discourage further violence and strengthen the power of British officials over the colonists. The colonists immediately labeled the measures the "Intolerable Acts." It soon became clear that England meant to enforce these "Intolerable Acts" and appointed General Thomas Gage, leader of the armed forces in America, as the governor of Massachusetts and sent him reinforcements to help maintain order. Great Britain, intending to punish Massachusetts as a warning to the other colonies, succeeded only in arousing antagonism throughout America.

The assembly of Massachusetts called for a continental congress, a proposal that was well received by all colonies. They chose representatives and convened on September 5, 1774, in Philadelphia. This was the First Continental Congress, and George Washington and Patrick Henry from Virginia, and Samuel Adams and John Adams from Massachusetts, were among its members. They passed resolutions setting out their grievances against the British government and adopted a boycott of British goods until there was a redress of those grievances. The boycott was, of course, a violation of British law.

In response to these demands England made one concession, with conditions attached: it was willing to exempt any colony from taxation that would bear its share of the imperial military and pay for supporting the officers of the Crown within its borders. With this concession Parliament pledged full support to the king in enforcing British laws in the colonies.

Shortly thereafter, General Gage, in Boston, sent a small force of soldiers toward Lexington and Concord in April 1775 for the purpose of seizing some military supplies supposedly being stored in that neighborhood. A small number of American militiamen, having been warned by William Dawes and Paul Revere, gathered on the green at Lexington early in the morning of April 19. Seeing that armed resistance would be futile, the captain of the militia ordered his men to disperse. A shot was fired. By whom no one knows, but militiamen poured in from the surrounding area and harassed the British troops on their retreat to Boston. This shot "heard around the world" announced the war for independence that followed.

By June a committee that included Thomas Jefferson, John Adams, Benjamin Franklin, and others was busy framing a document that was to express the ideals and spirit of independence. A draft was first prepared by Jefferson, a young Virginian, who would eventually be America's third president.

With the aid of Franklin and Adams, Jefferson, in flowing eloquence, laid out the justification for the War of Independence. There were three principal elements: (1) All men are created equal and endowed by their Creator with certain unalienable rights, among which are life, liberty, and the pursuit of happiness. (2) To secure those rights governments are instituted, and they derive their just powers from the consent of the governed. (3) When any form of government becomes destructive of these ends, it is the right of the people to alter or abolish it, and to institute a new government.

This "Declaration of Independence" is one of the fundamental documents of American history and electrified the American colonists' minds and hearts. Equally important, to other governments then existing around the world, it offered a revolutionary challenge. When this document was adopted, no true democratic republics existed anywhere. The French Revolution was not to occur until 1790. Most Americans favored independence from Britain, but some were afraid that "the people" might set up a government that could threaten their class privileges. (It is doubtful that the words "the people" were meant to refer to women, and they certainly did not apply to African slaves.) Some Loyalists—or Tories—did not want to separate from Great Britain and were now regarded as traitors in their own land. Tories included a high proportion of people with wealth and influence—merchants, lawyers, and landowners. The leaders of the revolution such as Washington, Adams, and Jefferson, however, were members of the same class. This was not a revolution of the poor, uneducated, and disposed, and most of the "founding fathers" were men of education and property. Many were slave owners.

Initial prospects for ultimate victory in the war were gloomy, with some battles won and some lost by each side. After abandoning Philadelphia to the British, Washington was forced to retire westward with his shattered troops to Valley Forge for the winter of 1777–78. Appearing to be almost at the end of his resources, news came that the British General John Burgoyne, who had invaded northern New York from Canada, was defeated at Saratoga. Burgoyne had expected to split the Americans militarily into two parts, but he failed miserably when British troops sent up from New York City did not arrive.

Burgoyne's surrender in 1777 marked a turning point in the war. It demonstrated that American troops, though poorly trained and supplied, had a genius for guerrilla warfare and that they could cope with British regulars. The victory at Saratoga was also critical because it helped the French to decide to enter the war against its rival, Britain. The alliance with France brought the kind of assistance the Americans needed: strong naval forces, generous loans, and a body of well-trained French officers and soldiers.

The alliance with France allowed the Americans to continue fighting the war against superior forces but did not bring immediate victory. In May 1780 the British took Charleston, South Carolina, and defeated the rebels in several North Carolina battles. The British commander Lord Charles Cornwallis next took his troops to Virginia in March 1781, where he tried to capture the American forces led by the young Frenchman, the Marquis de Lafayette, who had come to help in the struggle for independence. Failing in that attempt at great cost in men and supplies, Cornwallis drew back to the coast at Yorktown and waited for the British Navy to reinforce him from the sea. By that action he unwittingly sealed his doom and eventually brought an end to the war.

General Washington and his French allies, then in the North planning an attack on New York, saw an unexpected opportunity for a conclusive stroke at Yorktown. American and French troops were rushed south to pen up Cornwallis from the land side. A French fleet arrived from the West Indies in time to beat off British naval forces and prevent an escape by sea. Under fire from land and sea, Cornwallis surrendered on October 19, 1781. As events were to prove, the war was over. Stunned by the blow, the British government decided not to undertake another effort to recover its dominion over the colonies. The final treaty between the United States and Great Britain was signed on September 3, 1783, and ratified by the Congress in January 1784.

As the revolt against Great Britain proceeded to victory, a civil revolution within the American society took place. A large portion of the upper class collapsed, and after the British governors and their officials fled, thousands of Loyalist merchants, clergy, landlords, and lawyers were also forced to leave the country. Many large estates owned by British subjects were confiscated and sold off in blocks to Americans. The English Anglican Church was disestablished as the official church, and religious liberty was generally widened.

During the war, the Second Continental Congress had drafted and debated a proposed new form of government for the colonies should the patriots win. A plan called the Articles of Confederation was finally approved and sent to the state legislatures for review and adoption.

In colonial times, the British government had exercised control over all the colonies in essential matters of public policy and administration. It had conducted foreign affairs and provided common defense against other nations. The colonies were now states, each with its own legislature, but there was no central government.

There were heated debates over what changes should be made to the Articles of Confederation, which loosely linked the new United States together in what the document called "a firm league of friendship between the States." The Confederacy had a Congress but no chief executive or machinery to enforce the laws it passed. It had no judiciary empowered to try persons violating its laws or settle disputes among the States. It had no power to regulate commerce between the States, establish a single uniform currency for the country, or conduct foreign affairs.

Alexander Hamilton of New York persuaded a convention of five states to adopt a resolution urging the Congress of the United States to hold a convention at Philadelphia for the purpose of proposing amendments to the Articles of Confederation. Congress agreed, and in response all of the states except Rhode Island elected delegates, fifty-five in all. Many were the most prominent names in America, including George Washington, Benjamin Franklin, Alexander Hamilton, and James Madison.

In May 1787 the convention assembled and quickly put aside the task of amending the inadequate Articles of Confederation in favor of drafting an entirely new constitution creating a central government for the people of the United States of America. It met from May to September 17, 1787. Each of the states was "sovereign" and already had the power to decide all its own affairs. But for their fledgling country to survive in the world, the delegates realized there would have to be a "national" or federal government that would be more than a collection of different states, each with its own government. It would have to be something bigger and stronger. To accomplish this goal, each of the states would have to give up some of its "sovereign" powers. There were good reasons to fear a powerful new government with a central headquarters outside of one's state. A war had just been fought over that issue. The states were all different from one another in size and wealth. If they were to all be equal, the more numerous poor states might force the few rich states like New York and Virginia to share their wealth. On the other hand, if they were unequal and had power in proportion to their size or wealth, the small poor states had much to fear.

The framers considered only a republican form of government. (The term *democracy* was avoided because it was considered too inflammatory at the time.) They knew they could not possibly propose a monarch or a government ruled by an aristocracy. Their goal was to form some sort of federal government that would bind the thirteen states into a lasting union. There was no contemporary model to follow. England, in the mid-1600s, had experienced Oliver Cromwell's overthrow and execution of its king and attempted a republic that failed miserably and quickly reverted to monarchy. The future French Revolution, inspired in part by the current American Revolution, would fail as a republic and instead produce Emperor Napoleon. (At this time, Sweden was ruled by a hereditary king and powerful nobles along with a weak four-chamber parliament.) The framers were leaping into the unknown and they knew it.

The Constitutional Convention debated throughout the summer of 1787 and by September ultimately produced the Constitution of the United States, which (with relatively few amendments) lives today.

There would be two fundamentally equal legislative bodies. To reflect the power of the people, the House of Representatives would be elected every two years by the enfranchised voters in each state based on population. To protect the smaller states from their fear of being overwhelmed by the larger states, there would be two senators from each state regardless of population elected to six-year terms. The chief executive, the president, would be elected indirectly for four years by all the people qualified to vote. An independent Supreme Court, above all federal and state courts, would be appointed for life by the president with the consent of the Senate. This was not an ideal democracy of one-man, one-vote, but it permitted the survival of a nascent democracy in the dangerous world of aggressive monarchies, and importantly, provided a framework on which to build. It fell short of ideal, but as George Washington declared at the time, it was about as good as could be expected, and the people should adopt it, leaving to the future the making of corrections and amendments.

There was extensive public debate over the adoption of the proposed constitution, which had to be ratified by individual state conventions. It was finally ratified by all thirteen states in the spring of 1790. A bill of rights in the form of ten amendments guaranteeing specific civil rights was joined to the Constitution when the new government, under President George Washington, got under way. But none of these amendments affected the form of that government.

George Washington, the military leader of the War of Independence, was the logical choice to become the first president. If ever a man deserved to be called "Father of His Country," that man was George Washington. He combined military experience with infinite patience and determination, a sound sense of organization, absolute integrity, and regard for justice that even his rivals had to admit reflected a superiority of character. He exhibited no desire for personal glory or power. A sense of duty led Washington to take part in the Constitutional Convention after the war. That same sense of duty led him to accept the responsibilities of the first president of the United States of America. He refused to serve more than two terms, establishing an unwritten precedent that remained until Franklin Roosevelt was elected to a third term during World War II.

Washington's vice president, John Adams, a prominent "founding father," became the second president. He served one term until defeated by Thomas Jefferson in 1801. President Adams's most important appointment was the selection of John Marshall, a former congressman and secretary of state, as chief justice of the Supreme Court.

In forceful terms, Marshall ruled in a series of decisions that the Supreme Court had the sole power to determine what legislation, federal or state, was constitutional and enforceable. If found unconstitutional, these laws would be considered void and unenforceable. He also declared that the court had the power to reverse the decision of a state court upon appeal. In these decisions, Marshall strengthened the federal government at the expense of the states' autonomy. This helped to shape the loose collection of states into a more "national" union of the people. The power to nullify legislation as "unconstitutional" and to enforce "constitutional" rights has also given rise to many controversies throughout the history of the nation.

The U.S. Constitution said nothing about the formation of political parties. Washington was reelected by unanimous vote, but his vice president, John Adams, had opposition, a candidate sponsored by Thomas Jefferson and his followers, who were known as Republicans. Another faction, or party, the Federalists, had arisen led by Alexander Hamilton, Washington's secretary of the treasury.

To his partisans, Thomas Jefferson represented the small farmers and stood against the rich and well born. Hamilton and his Federalists appealed to the business interests and advocates of a strong and stable central government. Jefferson won the election and became the third president.

Shortly after he was elected, Jefferson received an offer he could not refuse from France's Emperor Napoleon Bonaparte. News reached Jefferson that the huge Louisiana Territory, extending from the Mississippi River to the Pacific Coast, had been ceded to France by Spain. Fearing that France might close the port of New Orleans to the shipment of American grain and farm products, Jefferson sent a special emissary to Napoleon authorized to buy New Orleans for $10 million if possible.

Even before the emissary arrived, Napoleon had concluded that he might lose his American possessions in a pending war with Britain and had told the American minister in Paris that he would sell the whole territory, including New Orleans, to the United States for $15 million. Thus, at one astonishing stroke and without warfare, the territory of the United States was more than doubled.

So little was known about this new land that Jefferson sponsored the expedition headed by Meriwether Lewis and William Clark to explore it, find an overland route to the Pacific, and report on its resources. On May 14, 1804, they set out on the Missouri River for the Northwest and reached what would become Montana. With the guidance in part by a Shoshone Indian woman named Sacagawea, the group made its hazardous way across the Rocky Mountains to the headwaters of the Columbia River, down which they floated swiftly to the Pacific Ocean by November 1805. They returned home more quickly and were back in St. Louis, having completed the journey of eight thousand miles in two years and four months. The report they compiled and published gave Americans anxious to move to the far Northwest considerable new knowledge.

The early 1800s saw the beginning of the Industrial Revolution that swept across Europe and the United States. With the invention and development of power-driven machines, more manufacturing was done in factories and less in homes and small shops. Machinery, driven first by water power and later by steam engines, was used to produce goods in great factories, swiftly and cheaply on a large scale.

All the additional fourteen states admitted to the Union between 1789 and 1840 differed from the original seaboard states, which had colonial backgrounds. In none of them was there an upper class of wealth and power comparable to the large land-owners and rich merchants of the original thirteen. There was clearly more equality in wealth and social conditions in the new agricultural states than in the old. The new states all adopted suffrage for all white men or with some slight qualifications on the right to vote and hold office.

In the spring of 1831, a twenty-six-year-old Frenchman, Alexis de Tocqueville, was sent by his government to study the prison system in America. He expanded his assignment to a study of this fascinating new democracy. In his extensive travels he observed the manners and habits, the industries and occupations, the day-to-day life of the people. When he returned to France, he described what he had seen in a book appropriately titled *Democracy in America*. This book remains one of the most perceptive studies of the young American nation.

De Tocqueville was enormously impressed with the rapid expansion of the new nation and the vitality of the people. "This gradual and continuous progress of the European race toward the Rocky Mountains has the solemnity of a providential event, he wrote. "It is like a deluge of men rising unabatedly and daily driven onward by the hand of God."

But the fact that struck Tocqueville most was the lack of class distinctions: "Amongst the novel objects that attracted my attention during my stay in the United States, nothing struck me more forcibly than the general equality of conditions."

He continued: "It is evident to all alike that a great democratic revolution is going on amongst us; but there are two opinions as to its nature and consequences. To some it appears to be a novel accident, which may still be checked; to others it seems irresistible, because it is the most uniform, the most ancient, and the most permanent tendency which is to be found in history."

In 1828, political and social democracy scored a major victory with the election of Andrew Jackson as president. In those days, the word "Democrat" was a radical term, seldom adopted publicly by politicians. This changed after Jackson was elected by defeating John Quincy Adams, the son of John Adams, the second president.

Before 1829, all of the presidents had come from surroundings of wealth and refinement. In contrast, Andrew Jackson had been born into poverty and had risen through his own efforts to a position of influence. He was identified with the hopes and ambitions of a majority of the people, and they claimed him for their own.

Jackson's election demonstrated that the western section of the country was a new force to be reckoned with. He was from Tennessee, the first president to be elected from a state that did not border on the Atlantic. Now for the first time a frontiersman, a westerner, was president.

CHAPTER 5

The United States: Lincoln, Civil War, Reconstruction

T HE NEXT TRULY GREAT PRESIDENT of the United States was Abraham Lincoln. In his lifetime, he saw the full impact of the Industrial Revolution, the creation of a "Cotton Economy" in the Southern states, the westward movement reach the Pacific, and the development of a strong antislavery movement that culminated in the Civil War.

Lincoln, born in a log cabin in Kentucky in 1809, educated himself, moved to Illinois, and after a tough struggle against poverty won some local renown as a trial lawyer. He served in the Illinois legislature and for one term in Congress. As he approached fifty, he was unknown except as a local politician-lawyer. His opportunity to gain national attention came when he was nominated by the new Republican Party to serve as a candidate for the United States Senate against the incumbent Stephen A. Douglas. Douglas was a nationally known Democrat with presidential ambitions and expected to become the Democrats' candidate in 1860 if he won the Illinois Senate seat. The campaign featured a series of debates that were reported by newspapers in every region of the land. Lincoln, gifted with a down-to-earth sense of humor and wit, was a match for Douglas in logical argument and general ability. He was not an abolitionist, but he believed that slavery was morally wrong. He accepted the basic principle of the new Republican Party that slavery should not be extended any further as new states entered the union. Douglas won the Senate election, but Lincoln gained national recognition and made a favorable impression on those who read about him, along with the thousands who heard him debate.

By 1860, the issue of slavery split many ties between North and South, including several church groups. The political parties were likewise divided. The Democrats split in two, one group nominating John C. Breckenridge of Kentucky for president and the other group nominating Stephen A. Douglas of Illinois. Making the most of the Democrats' division, the Republican convention meeting in Chicago named Abraham Lincoln as its candidate and adopted a platform plank opposed to the extension of slavery into the new territories. To make a wider appeal to particular voters, they adopted a plank favoring a protective tariff to encourage the development of "the industrial interests of the whole country." Another plank advocated a homestead law giving free land to settlers in the western territories. That pleased the thousands of Democrats who had supported the Homestead Bill of 1859, which the Democratic president, James Buchanan, had vetoed.

There were four parties running in the presidential campaign of 1860. Lincoln won a clear plurality, carrying all of the free (Northern) states except New Jersey. This marked the true birth of the Republican Party as a national party.

News of Lincoln's election caused South Carolina to call for a convention that was held in December 1860; delegates voted unanimously to withdraw South Carolina from the Union. Other Southern states followed. In February, a new union, the Confederate States of America, was formed, a constitution was created, and Jefferson Davis, a Mississippi planter, was elected its president.

James Buchanan remained president, but took no action, leaving that to Lincoln, who was not inaugurated until March 4, 1861. Lincoln attempted conciliation, and in his inaugural address he declared that no state could lawfully secede under the Constitution and that slavery was legal in the states where it was established and would not be disturbed. Thus far, no act of violence had been committed. For more than a month, uncertainty prevailed while representatives of both sides sought to reach a compromise or settlement of some kind, but ultimately, without success.

The spark that ignited the war was the Confederate bombardment on April 12 of Fort Sumter, situated on a little island in the harbor of Charleston, South Carolina, that remained garrisoned by federal troops. The flag of the United States flying above Federal troops had been fired upon. The effect was electric! Millions of people in the North who had been lukewarm or hesitant now were ready to fight. On April 15, Lincoln issued a call for troops and for a special session of Congress. In the South, the firing on Fort Sumter and Lincoln's call for troops caused immediate response. Two days later, on April 17, Virginia seceded from the Union. Arkansas, Tennessee, and North Carolina soon followed. But the South was far from "solid" in the desire to leave the Union. In Virginia, western counties were so opposed to it that they withdrew and later entered the Union as the state of West Virginia.

When war began in full force, the Confederacy had eleven states on its side against twenty-three states in the North. Nine million people in the South, more than one-third of them slaves, were aligned against 22 million people in the Northern states, which were rich in both agricultural and manufacturing resources. Southern strength appeared inferior, but the South, led by many officers who had been trained at West point and served in the U.S. Army prior to the Civil War, soon demonstrated ingenuity and enterprise in the art of warfare.

The North had a clear superiority in producing munitions and other war supplies, which increased as the war went forward. Shipping lanes to Great Britain and Europe remained open throughout the war. On the other hand, the South was blockaded from receiving almost all imports of iron, steel, munitions, and other goods. As the Federal blockade of Southern ports grew tighter, Confederate armies and the civilian population sank into dire distress. The Confederacy struggled to achieve recognition as an independent government, to win financial assistance, to break the blockade, and, if possible, gain direct intervention by Great Britain and France. The sympathies of the British aristocracy and government, the ruling classes in France, and Napoleon III, emperor of France, were overwhelmingly on the side of the South. But working people in English cities held mass meetings protesting giving assistance to slave owners; and Queen Victoria counseled her cabinet to be cautious. If it had not been for the decisive Union victories at Gettysburg and Vicksburg in the summer of 1863, British and French intervention might have come. In all events, Britain and France never recognized the independence of the Confederacy, nor did they ever intervene.

The most celebrated of all Lincoln's war measures was the Proclamation of Emancipation on January 1, 1863. The proclamation, issued under his war powers, declared all the slaves in the Confederate states to be free. From one point of view, this was an empty threat. In fact, it freed no slaves. In the loyal states of the Union, slaves remained slaves and in the district still controlled by Confederate arms, slaves also remained slaves. But the Proclamation electrified the imagination of all who loved liberty and was the signal move toward the abolition of slavery throughout the United States.

At the start of the war, the Confederacy had about 400,000 men under arms, large stores of supplies, and were better prepared for battle than the Union. The South became committed to fighting a defensive war on the theory that there remained some slight hope for compromise, and if heavy fighting did begin, the Northern armies would be defeated or worn down and eventually forced to accept the independence of the Confederacy.

The army of Northern Virginia under General Robert E. Lee remained powerful and confident. Lee felt so sure of his strength that he invaded Pennsylvania in the summer of 1863, hoping to drive a wedge into the Union and deal a fatal blow to the Northern war effort. At Gettysburg on July 3, 1863, Lee staked the fate of his army and, as it turned out, the Confederacy itself on a powerful bid for victory. Led by General George Pickett, 16,000 of Lee's finest soldiers charged up Cemetery Ridge through the devastating fire of Union troops. For a brief dramatic moment, the Confederate battle flag appeared on the crest of the ridge. But the Union forces were too strong, and the broken remnants of Pickett's men fell back. The next day Lee started his sorrowful but skillful retreat back to Virginia.

The beginning of the end of the war came in 1864, when General Grant was put in charge of all of the Federal armies. In May of 1864, he assumed responsibility for the Virginia Campaign and started a relentless drive on the Confederate capital, Richmond, sparing neither men nor resources. That same month, General William T. Sherman began his march from Chattanooga through Georgia to Atlanta. After taking Atlanta, Sherman led his army on a march across Georgia to Savannah, burning and destroying as he went.

On December 20, Savannah crumpled and Sherman's army turned northward to South Carolina and into North Carolina and toward Virginia. The war was drawing to a finish. On April 3, 1865, Grant took Richmond, which President Jefferson Davis had abandoned in a hurried flight. Lee took his unbeaten army westward with Grant in pursuit and General Philip Sheridan on his flank.

On April 9, bereft of hope, Lee surrendered at the small village of Appomattox Court House in Virginia.

When they met, Lee handed his sword to Grant. Lee was in full dress uniform. Grant was in a private's unbuttoned blouse. Grant offered Lee generous terms. He took no prisoners and allowed Lee's men to return to their homes with the promise that they would not again take up arms against the Union. The troops had to surrender their weapons, but Grant permitted Lee's officers to keep their pistols and swords.

The meeting concluded, Lee mounted his horse and rode off. The Union troops started to cheer. Grant ordered them to be silent, saying, "The war is over; the rebels are our countrymen again."

Thus, the war that started with the bombardment of Fort Sumter came to an end.

During the war, a constitutional amendment, building upon Lincoln's Emancipation Proclamation, was introduced in Congress abolishing slavery throughout the United States. After prolonged discussions, it passed both houses by the requisite two-thirds vote and was sent to the states for ratification, coming into effect in December 1865. Thus the verbal emancipation proclaimed by Lincoln in 1863 under his war powers was extended to include all slaves, North and South, and became imbedded in the U.S. Constitution as the Thirteenth Amendment.

In addition to Lincoln's leadership in freeing the slaves and successfully prosecuting the war, his brief speech honoring the dead killed in the battle of Gettysburg has had an enormous historic effect on the American nation. At that time, true democracy had not yet been achieved. Women, African Americans, and Indians could not fully participate in self-government. But Lincoln's words took the country beyond the statement in the Declaration of Independence that "all men are created equal" and made it clear "that this nation, under God, shall have a new birth of freedom; and that *government of the people, by the people, for the people,* shall not perish from the earth." This simple description of democracy became the goal aspired to by masses around the world and gives us enduring direction today.

When Lincoln was reelected in November 1864, he had a new vice president, Andrew Johnson, a former Democrat. In his Second Inaugural Address, Lincoln was preparing the country for a peace of reconciliation when he said:

> With malice toward none, with charity for all; with firmness in the right, as God gives us to see the right; let us strive on to finish the work we are in; to bind up the nation's wounds; to care for him who shall have borne the battle, and for his widow, and his orphan—to do all which may achieve and cherish a just and lasting peace among ourselves and with all nations.

Before he could fulfill his promise, Lincoln died tragically on April 15, 1865, at the hands of an assassin.

The presidency passed to Andrew Johnson, who adopted Lincoln's conciliatory attitude toward the defeated South. Not all leaders of the Republican Party saw eye to eye with Lincoln and Johnson on their ideas about the reconstruction of the Union. One group within the party, called "Radical Republicans," wanted to punish the South and leave no stone unturned in seeing that justice was accorded the former slaves. The Radical Republicans developed their own severe program of reconstruction.

Congress set the conditions each former Confederate state had to meet before being readmitted to the Union. They were divided into military districts under the control of a northern army officer given power to keep order and supervise the process of reconstruction.

No state could be readmitted to the Union until it had ratified the Fourteenth Amendment, which gave all former slaves citizenship. The amendment declared that all persons born in the United States are citizens of the United States and of the state where they reside and no state shall deprive any person of "life, liberty or property, without due process of law," nor deny any person "equal protection of the laws." In addition, all former congressmen and state officials who had joined the Confederacy were disqualified from holding state or federal offices. For a brief period, the governments of the Southern states were in the hands of Negro men, white men who had not been disenfranchised for supporting the Confederacy, and "carpetbaggers" who came from the North after the war seeking opportunities. Northerners actually held most of the important political offices, at least in the early postwar years.

Disenfranchised white men and other white voters, indignant at the new regime, quickly set about overthrowing it. They used legal arguments and illegal threats to keep blacks from voting. Secret societies, such as the Ku Klux Klan, terrorized blacks and their white sympathizers. In state after state, "white supremacy" was reestablished. Social chaos reigned. The Southern economy, dependent on slave labor, was torn apart by the four-year war. Everywhere the former slaves, some 4 million in number, were free at last, but free to do what? Most were uneducated and had never owned land. Most of their former owners could not pay them wages because Confederate money was worthless and U.S. currency was almost nonexistent in the South. Disease due to hunger and lack of sanitation swept across the South. Thousands of people died during the summer and winter of 1865–66.

White Southerners blamed the Republican Party for the war, which was fought principally in the South, as well as for the loss of life and property, the loss of their economy, and the humiliating postwar "reconstruction." It is small wonder that in reaction the Southern states became the "Solid South" for the Democratic Party for over 100 years.

The chaos and turmoil in the country took its toll on the presidency. Early in 1868, animosity toward President Johnson, caused by deep disagreements with Congress, reached such a pitch that the House of Representatives impeached him. A trial before the Senate was held, and Johnson escaped conviction and removal from office by a margin of only one vote.

The elimination of slavery was only the first step in African Americans' long march toward genuine freedom and equality. That struggle continued through the next century and continues today in more nuanced ways.

While the Southern people were struggling among social and economic ruins, the Northern economy was expanding with unprecedented speed. In the decade after the war nearly 7 million persons were added to the population of the country, counting new immigrants. But the increase in the North and the West was far greater than in the South.

The entire country, however, continued its geographical expansion. In 1867, the territory of Alaska was purchased from Russia. An intercontinental railroad stretching from the East Coast to California was completed in 1869. Land was free to homestead settlers, and large tracts of land were obtained legally and sometimes illegally by mining companies and speculators. Fortunes were made by some as the frontier pushed westward and the continent started to fill up.

The advance of settlers and the conquest of Indians in the Great Plains of mid-America took place after the Civil War. Here, ruled the buffalo, as well as seminomadic Indian tribes, such as the Sioux, Blackfeet, Crow, and Cheyenne, and their horses. Between 1865 and 1886 there was constant violent conflict between the whites and the Indians. In these campaigns, soldiers who had fought on opposite sides in the Civil War, including black troops, now fought together against the Indians. As they were compressed, the Indians fought back fiercely to hold on to their lands and distinctive way of life. During this period, three transcontinental railways were completed that drew people west with greater speed and safety than the covered wagon. It also drew white hunters who slaughtered the herds of buffalo that the Indians were dependent upon for food, clothing, and shelter.

The westward expansion of white America caused constant collisions with various Indian tribes, who for generations had lived as hunter-gatherers dependent upon vast tracts of natural land belonging to all tribal members. The very idea of private, exclusive ownership of land, so essential to farmer-settlers, was unknown to Indian cultures. The clash of these two societies was inevitable, although sometimes peaceful accommodation was possible. But the powerful pressure for acquisition, and the expectation of new land by farmers, speculators, and developers, aided by the government, nearly always ended in the removal of Indians to less desirable land. This was accomplished through Indian "wars" and treaties negotiated with individual tribes—treaties that were inevitably broken by whites. This Indian "removal," as it was often called, cleared the land from the Appalachians to the Mississippi River for growing cotton in the South and grain in the North. In 1820, 120,000 Indians lived east of the Mississippi, but by 1844, fewer than 30,000 were left.

Guns, particularly revolvers that allowed multiple shots in fighting, railroads, and broken treaties worked together to sweep the Indians from the Great Plains into remote reservations. It was President Rutherford B. Hayes himself who said to Congress in 1877, "Many, if not most, of our Indian wars have had their origin in broken promises and acts of injustice on our part."

In addition to postwar geographic expansion, there was industrial, commercial, and financial expansion taking place. Concentration in industrial enterprise took place with the help of large banks. Great new associations of capital were formed, such as the J. P. Morgan Company with the New York Central Railroad Company and the United States Steel Company.

The concentration of wealth gave rise to associations of labor groups. The American Federation of Labor, a national union of crafts, was organized in 1886. The organizations clung to a program of standard hours and wages, fair conditions of labor, and collective bargaining with employees. It accepted the capitalistic system of ownership and sought to improve the position of labor, especially skilled labor, within that framework. No labor political party, per se, was formed.

In no period of American history was change more disrupting than in the generation following the Civil War. The major cause of these changes was the rapid growth of industry after the war. New power-driven machinery was installed in factories, giant corporations were organized, and new methods of mass production were developed. All helped the American people to raise their standard of living, but this bright picture was not without some dark shadows. For example, cities grew and became overcrowded, which created new problems. "Big business" grew, but extremes of poverty and wealth were created. Expanding industries brought vast wealth to a few owners. While some wage earners were doing very well, the majority, while better off than industrial workers in Europe, were living in near poverty. In 1892, the demand for reform reached clamorous proportions from small-business owners, wage earners, and especially the western farmers. A tax on income was proposed, which provoked violent debate in Congress but was ultimately enacted into law in 1894. In 1895 the U.S. Supreme Court declared it unconstitutional, by a vote of five to four, as a "direct tax" that had to be apportioned among the states. Most citizens considered this decision as one more example of how the government favored "big business" and helped fan the flame of protest that was sweeping the country. The federal income tax was authorized in 1913 by the Sixteenth Amendment to the Constitution.

For over three centuries Americans, as they called themselves, had concentrated on expansion and development of their new country. The foreign policy of the United States, as enunciated by Washington in his Farewell Address, in Jefferson's messages, and the Monroe Doctrine, was based on the proposition that "foreign entanglements" should be avoided. The constant wars and squabbles of Europe were especially anathema, and territories beyond easy reach were not to be sought. It was not until thirty years after the Civil War that some American politicians and writers began to plan and publicly talk about a reversal of this policy and urge the transformation of the United States into a "great World Power" such as England, France, and Spain.

Best known of these influential new imperialists was a vigorous young New York Republican, Theodore Roosevelt. Another was an American naval officer, Alfred Mahan, who advocated mightily for the building of a big navy and expansion of worldwide commerce. Another agitator for plunging into world-power politics was Josiah Strong, a militant Protestant missionary. In his book, *Our Country,* Strong declared that the Untied States was in peril of socialism, that the Anglo-Saxon race was chosen by God to civilize the world, and that the major responsibility for this work fell to the people of the United States. Republican senator Henry Cabot Lodge, from Massachusetts, strongly supported this imperialist agenda in Congress and was an important friend of Mahan and Roosevelt.

A test of this new plan for entrance into worldwide politics came during President McKinley's administration in the late 1890s. For years, Cuba had been torn by revolts against Spanish domination, and a new rebellion had flared up in 1895. In early 1898, an American battleship, the *Maine,* was sent to Havana "to safeguard American interests" and was blown up by an explosion in which 260 U.S. sailors lost their lives. The origin of this disaster was never established, but Americans (who were overwhelmingly sympathetic to the cause of Cuban independence) held Spanish officials responsible. In a war resolution, Congress declared that Cuba should become free and independent. To fend off any attempt by the imperialists to annex the island, Congress added the Platt Amendment, which said, "The United States hereby disclaims any disposition or intention to exercise sovereignty, jurisdiction, or control over said island." War began ostensibly only to free Cuba from Spain, and ended doing that. But in addition, the United States acquired Spain's island of Puerto Rico in the Caribbean and the Philippine Islands in the Far East.

The American forces quickly eliminated the Spanish navy and army in and about Cuba and occupied Puerto Rico without a battle. Meanwhile, the American fleet, under Admiral George Dewey, destroyed the Spanish war vessels in the harbor of Manila on May 1, 1898, effectively ending Spanish rule in the Philippines.

In the final treaty drawn up in Paris, independence was granted to Cuba; Puerto Rico and Guam were ceded to the United States; and the Philippines were transferred to the United States for $20 million. Unrelated to the conflict with Spain, the Hawaiian Islands were annexed by the United States and became a territory in 1900.

The United States had suddenly become an imperial world power that acquired land beyond its borders directly from another imperial power by war or purchase, while the wishes of the native people are considered inconsequential.

In the nineteenth century, the United States underwent growth, transformation, and bloody conflicts. The twentieth century promised more of the same.

CHAPTER 6

Sweden in the 1800s

A T THE BEGINNING of the nineteenth century, the United States finished shedding its role as a collection of royal colonies and was becoming a federal republic of semisovereign states. Sweden, too, was slowly evolving toward democracy. Europe continued to be embroiled in wars as the French emperor, Napoleon, sought to extend his empire across the continent, while Sweden remained an imperial monarchy in the Baltic region of Europe. Thomas Jefferson was elected president in 1801 and in 1803 purchased the Louisiana Territory from France. Napoleon declared himself emperor of France in 1804. In its last European war, Sweden's territory of Finland was invaded and annexed in 1808 by Russia.

War weariness and divisions among the nobles made further resistance impossible, forcing Sweden to accept Russian terms of peace, by which Sweden lost a full third of its territory, including all of Finland. It was a drastic amputation of its kingdom and led to the overthrow of King Gustav IV Adolph. The loss of Finland, which separated people who had developed together for centuries and shared a common culture, was a severe and traumatic shock to the Swedes.

In 1809 a group of rebel nobles in the Riksdag (Parliament) dethroned the Swedish king and met to decide upon a new one. They eventually turned to France and chose Jean-Baptiste Bernadotte, one of Napoleon's talented young field marshals. Bernadotte came north to Sweden in 1810, conveniently converting to Lutheranism, and became Karl XIV Johan. This new line of hereditary monarchs continues to the present day. When the old king was ousted and a new one recruited from France, there was no longer any vestige of divine rights. Any power the king acquired came by his election, which required the approval of the Rikstag that was dominated by the Nobel estate.

Also in 1809, the Riksdag set about creating a written constitution that, although extensively amended, would remain in force until 1974. It was actually more a written recitation of historical customs followed to that date than a formulation of a new plan of government. It confirmed that there was an independent judiciary with a highest court having power to declare acts of the Riksdag inconsistent with the constitution. Yet that court lacked real power, like that of the U.S. Supreme Court, to invalidate laws as unconstitutional, for it could be overruled by the Riksdag at its next session. Appointments to high positions were to be based on merit alone, thus presumably eliminating some positions held by nobles based only on heredity. The king's powers were limited, but it was clear that he would remain a ruling monarch who could introduce and veto legislation, appoint ministers who made up the council of state, and direct foreign policy. Throughout the 1800s, Sweden could properly be classified as a constitutional monarchy — not yet a parliamentary democracy.

The Riksdag met at least once every three years or in special session, and had the right to initiate legislation, reject royal proposals, and, most important, control the budget and taxation. However, the medieval four-estate structure of the Riksdag (clergy, nobles, burghers, and farmers) remained. The Act of Succession and the Press Freedom Act completed the fundamental documents of the Swedish political system at that time. Through clever diplomacy, Karl XIV Johan forced Norway into a reluctant union that lasted until 1905. Norway, however, never became Swedish territory as had Finland and had always been more attached to Denmark than to Sweden.

Fueled by dramatic and revolutionary reforms taking place in France, England, and the United States, there was continued agitation in the Swedish press and among intellectuals to reform the Riksdag and increase voter suffrage. Knowing Sweden today, it is hard to imagine that less than 150 years ago it had a caste system so entrenched that the Rikstag was divided into four estates that represented only four social and occupational groups. People outside those groups had no voice in government. A program for reform of the four-estate structure of the Riksdag drew together all reform elements, including even some nobles who by midcentury had come to realize the necessity of change. It was then that Sweden had historic peaceful reform that occurred in 1865–66, at the same time the United States completed its Civil War.

The principal architect of this great reform of 1865–66 was Louis De Geer, a man of noble birth whose ancestors had come from Holland to Sweden six generations earlier and established a wealthy, prominent family. He studied law at Uppsala University, held judicial and other official positions, and participated in the Riksdags of 1853–54 and 1856–58. In 1858, the king, Karl XV, persuaded De Geer, then forty, to become his prime minister. (As such, there were no political parties at that time.) De Geer sensed the vital importance of constitutional reform of the Riksdag, so when the two lower estates, burghers and farmers, raised the question in the Riksdag, he made their cause his own. The proposal, drawn up by De Geer, was presented to all estates to be acted upon at the session in 1865. It called for elimination of the four estates and their replacement by a two-chamber parliament that would be elected by common vote and meet annually. The two houses were to be "of equal competence and authority," but were different in property qualifications and the people allowed to vote.

This was hardly a revolutionary proposal, but De Geer knew that only a relatively modest change had a chance to obtain the king's support and pass a vote in the Hall of Nobles.

De Geer's plan, eventually supported by the king, was put forward as a government proposition. It immediately gathered popular public approval. The press was overwhelmingly in favor, so it would come down to a vote by the nobles. That vote is vividly described by the distinguished historian Franklin D. Scott in his seminal book, *Sweden: The Nation's History*:

> Long before the day scheduled—Monday, the fourth of December 1865—eager reformers flocked into Stockholm by boat and carriage and train. Hotels were filled and restaurants and pubs became political discussion clubs. On that December Monday, crowds waited tensely outside the parliamentary halls. The farmers' Estate met at 9:00 A.M. and promptly, without debate, voted unanimously for the government's proposal. The burghess met in their hall at 10:00 A.M. all in full dress in honor of the occasion. One negative speech took forty-five minutes, four other members announced their opposition; then the vote was taken, and it was sixty to five in favor. The clergy would have voted no had they possessed the courage of their convictions, but they were afraid they might be the only Estate to oppose, and they dared not risk the popular reaction. Hence they met and decided merely to await the decision of the nobility. . . .
>
> Everything depended on the nobles, and their decision remained in doubt for four long days. Debate was vigorous but restrained. Every seat in the house was taken. The Hall of the Nobility was (and is) one of the architectural jewels of the country. Its walls were hung with the coat

of arms of ancient heroes, generals of the Thirty Years
War, and the great officials of the state. It was a handsome symbol of Sweden's Age of Greatness. Over 700
representatives of the foremost families of the land filled
the benches and the aisles and the window niches. From
nine until three on the first day the nobles bombarded
each other with speeches, blending argument and nostal-
gia. . . . And everyone was aware of the upswelling public
opinion.

At long last, at 2:00 P.M. on Thursday, the noble representatives of the old order filed up to drop their votes in the urns.
Counting was slow and hard to keep track of, but when it was
finished the tally surprised everyone: 361 *Ja* and 294 *Nej,* a margin
of 67 votes in favor. Scott continued his description of this vote
and its significance:

> The reform of 1865–66 marked a watershed. The old
> structure of government was a monarchic-aristocratic
> partnership with a participatory voice allowed to burghess
> and farmers. It had worked fairly well for several centu-
> ries. But in the mid-nineteenth century, Sweden was in
> the doldrums while Europe was edging its way into a new
> industrial era. Neither the personnel nor the structure
> of the old Swedish system was suited to these changing
> times. The nobles' dominance of political life and the
> archaic four-chamber parliament blocked the road to
> progress. Their elimination was a prerequisite for the
> attainment of democracy.
>
> One other relevant fact must be noted well: A fun-
> damental change had been brought about by peaceful
> means. The old order yielded sulkily but without threats

or violence. The reform was moderate enough that it could be accepted, and further change could evolve from there . . . the king had troops alerted for possible trouble. But there was no trouble, no sense of violence in the air. Reasonableness characterized the transition, and there was therefore no legacy of bitterness to poison the future.

The new Riksdag of two chambers was elected in the fall of 1866. It did not democratize Swedish politics, but it did open the door to the future. For better or for worse, plutocracy (rule by the rich) had replaced nobility. But less than 10 percent of the country's 2.5 million people had the right to vote because of gender and wealth requirements.

Sweden was well behind the United States as a functioning democracy by the late nineteenth century, but was more similar in its development to Denmark, Norway, and Great Britain and, like those countries, moving away from monarchy toward democratic parliamentarianism.

Even after 1866, the nobles maintained an importance based on tradition, education, and prestige. Family wealth and power came originally from land ownership, and later military and diplomatic service remained their stronghold similar to the aristocracy in Europe. Well into the twentieth century, this "upper class" has remained overrepresented in the student bodies of Uppsala and Lund universities, whose prestige is similar to America's Harvard, Yale, and Princeton and England's Oxford and Cambridge. (Interestingly, whatever it proves, our recent presidents in the United States, George Bush I and II, Bill Clinton, and candidate John Kerry are all graduates of Yale University.)

After the parliamentary reform in 1886, participation by eligible voters was very low. There were no political parties as there were in America to give voice to new issues and new interests as they arose. Nevertheless, society continued to change through industrialization, urbanization, education, and mobility and was generally divided among those who advocated continued change and those who preferred the present order. The reigning kings during this period naturally took a dim view of increased democracy, but grew to understand that they could do little to hold it back.

During the early nineteenth century, most Swedes lived in small villages and farms. In 1800, only two towns, Stockholm and Göteborg, had more than 10,000 people. Conditions were particularly bad for a small farmer who lost his land and was forced to become a sharecropper or a landless laborer. The displaced farmer lived with his family in a tiny shack in a rear field and worked, when he could, for the farmer or noble who owned the farm. There were serious problems of health, vagrancy, and begging.

Not until the 1880s and 1890s was there a turn for the better when industry started to grow and absorb some of the excess labor supply and emigration began to skim off more. The exodus from Sweden has been named the Great Migration. The young and unemployed were the ones who left for the United States, many from the over-populated, stony provinces of Småland in the south and Värmland in the west. It was during this time that my grandparents, as young people, crossed the Atlantic to establish a better home in America. My grandparents on my father's side came directly from Småland to Duluth in Minnesota in 1892, where their only child, my father, was born and lived his entire life. My grandparents on my mother's side immigrated somewhat later to Minnesota from Värmland and had six children. They, too, eventually settled in Duluth, where my parents met and were married in 1921.

My father's parents died before I was born, but I treasure my personal memories of my mother's parents (mormor and morfar), whom I knew only as a young child. Grandfather (morfar) was a tall, handsome, distinguished-looking man with a large mustache and silver-white hair who was always reading a Bible with extra large type, the words spoken by Jesus printed in red. A bricklayer by trade and a lay preacher in the Swedish Mission Covenant Church, he died when I was six years old. I was considered too young to attend his funeral but to this day regret my exclusion. His wife, my grandmother, was properly named Ingaborg, but we children called her "Tum Tum" for some unexplained reason. I always incorrectly assumed it meant "small and sweet and round" in Swedish.

Political parties in Sweden did not come into existence until the late 1860s. The Liberal Party became the cornerstone of the non-socialist left and represented a diverse range of intellectual and occupational groups who sought continued reform and advocated a political democracy and free market capitalism. The Conservative Party occupied the right of the political spectrum. This was the party of the old ruling elites and those who preferred order, stability, and legitimacy. A third party, the Social Democratic Workers' Party, founded in 1889, came from the growth of industrialization and the resulting working class. It eventually developed a national organization. Ideologically, the Social Democrats were left of the Liberal Party, but most of the party leaders then and now believed in gradual change of the political, economic, and social orders through peaceful means. One of the primary goals of both Liberals and Social Democrats was universal suffrage, which was not accomplished until after 1900.

Released from the burdens of constant wars, Sweden abandoned ambitions of empire and experienced population growth and change during the nineteenth century. Between 1800 and 1900, the population of Sweden rose from 2.4 million to 5.4 million. During the first half of the century, the economy moved from primarily agricultural to one more diverse, with mining, forestry, industrial, and trade elements. Although a small group of towns grew larger as important trade centers, change occurred slowly. Poverty continued to be widespread and rural life was backward for most. A few individuals enjoyed wealth and power, while most people remained extremely poor. After 1850, industrialization increased as it did in Europe and the United States. Old Sweden, primarily agricultural, local, and isolated, changed dramatically by 1900, but without the vast expanse of new land and enormous increase in population the United States experienced during that century.

The introduction of comprehensive, compulsory education was one of the most important changes that took place in the nineteenth century and greatly shaped Swedish society. Literacy rates had been relatively high in Sweden for centuries primarily because of the church's concern with the people's ability to read the Bible and literature of the faith. Confirmation in the state church required basic literacy. Before the 1840s, elementary education was mainly church-sponsored but scattered. Of course, the aristocratic elites had educated their children privately for years and reinforced a class society.

In 1842, a uniform compulsory school law was enacted that was designed to create a national system similar to those earlier enacted in Denmark (1814) and Norway (1827).

Under its terms, every rural and urban parish was to have at least one permanent school for boys and girls staffed by a trained teacher. School governance was to be under the control of a council headed by the local rector with costs met by a combination of taxes and fees. A national system, with wide local variations, gradually developed. The parliament continued to make revisions including two units, one for younger children, the other for older students (1858). Other revisions involved the establishment of a seven-year term for compulsory schooling (1880) and the extension of teacher training from three years to four (1863).

Curriculum in the lower schools focused on Christianity, Swedish, arithmetic, local history, work skills, singing, crafts, and games. The upper schools emphasized traditional subjects such as geometry, geography, natural science, history, art, and physical education. Young people learned what it meant to be "Swedish," and much of what students read, saw, and heard was strongly nationalistic. There was no wall of separation between church and state in public education. Higher education in Sweden experienced considerable growth in scale and diversity during the nineteenth century, but remained largely for the elites.

Swedish women have come a long way since 1800, when they were, like women in most European societies, subordinate to men. On the farms there was a degree of equality in their work in the fields alongside men, and they traditionally had the questionable honor of taking care of the cows and handling the keys. In the towns, however, they were servants of men. Unmarried women had practically no status or position, and few jobs were available to them other than as household servants. In 1846, women gained the right to work in commerce and crafts, and in 1853, to teach in primary schools. After 1858, unmarried women could be declared "of age" at twenty-five (boys at age twenty-one), which allowed them to marry and dispose of property without the permission of a guardian. Because there was a growing need for trained teachers, a women's teachers college was established in 1861. Next, in 1862, women were granted the right to vote in local elections but did not become eligible to run for municipal councils until 1909.

The growing realization that the country, by eliminating women's options, was losing valuable human resources was spurred by the writings of two Swedish authors in the mid-1800s. One was Carl Johas Almquist, who wrote a novel, *Sara Videbeck*, the story of a good-looking middle-class girl, thoroughly respectable, who falls in love with a young army sergeant she meets on a trip. Their mutual attraction leads to the girl's surprising proposal that they live together without any of the obligations of marriage, such as the expected round of household duties, with each partner preserving complete independence. The pleasant way the tale was told and the reasonableness of the characters brought the novel wide circulation. But the ideas it suggested horrified contemporary Swedes and led to Almquist's loss of position as a teacher and cleric and his eventual flight into exile in the United States. However, his blatant challenge to the institution of marriage and his call for greater freedom for women had a widespread impact.

Another proponent of women's rights was Fredrika Bremer, who wrote prolifically and effectively that women were the equals of men and ought to be educated and treated as such. Her emphasis was not only on rights and equality but on the right to vote and participate more fully in society because this would have a positive effect on men and all of society. She, of course, raised a storm of protest at the time, but personally having spent a lifetime in and observing public life and society, I believe she was completely correct and has been confirmed by modern Sweden.

By the end of the nineteenth century, Swedes had become more aware of their identity as one country and one culture rather than people from a certain local rural region. Compulsory public education, universal literacy, industrialization, urbanization, more mobility, and the renunciation of war set the stage for a remarkable twentieth century.

CHAPTER 7

Both Countries Grow Similar: 1900 to 1945

A T THE START of the twentieth century and before World War I, Sweden and the United States, although thousands of miles distant, were growing more and more similar. Industrialization had come in a rush to each country, and both had healthy and expanding compulsory education systems. The number of workers engaged in full-time farming was rapidly decreasing, especially in Sweden, while manufacturing and other trades and jobs were expanding as people moved from the farms to the cities. Democracy, in the sense of the equality of all citizens, had not fully arrived in either country. Sweden still had a class of nobles, and there was a heredity king with substantial governing power. The United States had acquired a small financial class, with well-known families such as the Rockefellers holding enormous wealth, while there was an existing underclass of ex-slaves, mainly in the South. For the most part, Native Americans had been relegated to reservations.

Sweden remained the smaller and poorer country, but the United States was experiencing an explosive growth. This attracted thousands of landless farm workers, like my ancestors, from southern and western Sweden to emigrate to North American in search of a better life. The Swedish author Vilhelm Moberg (1898–1973) is widely known for his quartet about this migration, *The Emigrants,*

Unto a New Land, The Settlers, and *The Last Letter Home.* (Two successful movies based on these books were made in the 1970s.)

The industrialization of both countries at the end of the nineteenth century and the first part of the twentieth century inevitably brought increased worker organization and a push for better conditions. But in neither country was there any serious talk of the revolutionary overthrow of the government as was soon to happen in Russia in 1917. Democracy had been sufficiently established in both countries to resolve most societal grievances peacefully.

A difference between the two countries in foreign affairs became evident at the turn of the century. By that time, Sweden had recognized that it would not be a "Great Power" and that peace and neutrality would serve it best. Russia grabbed its province of Finland in 1809 (Finland had been a part of Sweden for longer than parts of southern Sweden, which had been part of Denmark until comparatively recent historical times), and additional holdings in the Baltic and northern Europe had also been lost to the Germans. So when Norway chose to sever its dynastic connection with Sweden in 1905, the decision was accepted by the Swedes without a shot being fired. Like Canada and the United States, the two countries have remained on the closest of terms. While Sweden, the older country, was abandoning its past dreams of empire, the United States took its first significant steps toward becoming a "Great Power" when it started the Spanish-American War in 1898.

After the reelection of President William McKinley in 1900, and his almost immediate assassination, came the administrations of Theodore Roosevelt (1901–9), William H. Taft (1909–13) and Woodrow Wilson (1913–21). This early part of the twentieth century has been labeled by some as the Progressive Period. However, Theodore Roosevelt and Woodrow Wilson should be considered much more "progressive" than William Taft. Unionization was growing, but most members were white male skilled tradesmen in the American Federation of Labor (AFL), which represented 80 percent of all union membership. The number of women working outside the home grew slightly, but only one out of a hundred belonged to a union. More radical movements grew and reached out to the unorganized industrial workers and to blacks, who were snubbed by the AFL. Despite their small numbers, the Industrial Workers of the World, or "Wobblies," led by William "Big Bill" Haywood, became a threat to the new rich capitalist class. Another leading figure during this early period of social protest in America was Eugene Debs, who ran for president under the banner of the Socialist Party in 1904 and 1908; in 1912 he received almost a million votes, double what he had received in 1908.

Debs was later jailed when he spoke to an outdoor crowd in 1917, urging listeners to avoid fighting in World War I. Congress had passed the Espionage Act that year, making it a crime when the United States is at war (as it was) to cause or attempt to cause "refusal of duty in the military or naval forces of the United States, or . . . obstruct the recruiting or enlisted service of the U.S." In a passing nod to free speech the act had a clause that said, "Nothing in this section shall be construed to limit or restrict . . . any discussion, comment, or criticism of the acts or politics of the Government."

Nevertheless, Debs's wide-ranging 1917 speech was too strong and too critical for the jury and, later, the Supreme Court to swallow:

> "They tell us we live in a great free republic; that our institutions are democratic; that we are a free and self-governing people. That is too much even for a joke. . . .
>
> "Wars throughout history have been waged for conquest and plunder . . . and that is war in a nutshell. The

master class has always declared the wars; the subject
class has always fought the battles."

Debs refused to take the stand in his defense or call any wit-
nesses, but he didn't deny what he had said in his speech.

The jury found him guilty of violating the Espionage Act. He
was sentenced to ten years in prison but served thirty-two months.
Debs was sixty-six when he was released by President Warren G.
Harding in 1921.

Nothing similar happened in Sweden because that nation successfully avoided entry into the war, although there were those
who agitated for the war on the side of the Germans and against
Russia because it had "stolen" Finland and the Åland Islands from
them a century earlier. The king and some highly placed advisers
were pro-German, but Parliament and the cabinet were strongly
opposed and favored armed neutrality. By the end of the war,
Germany's submarine warfare, the entry of the United States,
and the ruthlessness of the war turned most Swedes to favor the
British, French, and American allies.

The two dominant political figures of this time of transition in
their respective countries were Theodore Roosevelt in America
and Hjalmar Branting in Sweden. Roosevelt, a Republican, was
the leading figure during the so-called Progressive Period in
America, and Branting was at the same time the nurturing parent
of the Social Democratic Party in Sweden. It is doubtful that they
ever had any personal contact. Roosevelt died of a heart attack
in 1919. He once said, "No president has ever enjoyed himself as
much as I have." Branting was the first Social Democrat elected to
the Rikstag in 1896 and went on to become the Social Democratic
prime minister three different times. He died in 1925.

Others provided the immediate initial spark that started the

Social Democratic Party, but it was Hjalmar Branting who tended the fire. The young Branting was so convinced of the need for social reform that he left the university without a degree to devote himself full time to the promotion of socialism. He accepted the Marxist belief in the class struggle, the materialistic interpretation of history, and the inevitable impoverishment of the masses that would prompt revolution. Yet with the passing of years and the changes accomplished through the political process, Branting moderated his views considerably. He could see that with advancing industrialization in Sweden there was no certainty that workers would inevitably become impoverished and unite in revolution.

Branting was a convinced socialist, but he was also an independent thinker and primarily a Swede, so he was not subservient to foreign ideologies. For example, agriculture in Sweden was not becoming centralized, and in a democracy the overwhelming numbers of small farmers could not be disregarded or classed together with the same interests that concerned the workers in the cities. Radical revolutionary rhetoric remained, but Branting and his Social Democrats turned their attention to improving the life of the poor in practical ways that led to workers' protective laws in 1912 and a general pension insurance in 1913. A social revolution by gradualism was making progress. The leaders of the Social Democrats and other left-leaning parties discovered that the king and conservative authorities wouldn't risk taking measures to block them, so they became convinced they could accomplish their objectives by working within the system.

Theodore Roosevelt was one of the great presidents of the United States, a reputation that earned his enshrinement on Mount Rushmore in South Dakota along with Washington, Jefferson, and Lincoln. He embodied the Progressive movement in America at the same time Hjalmar Branting and his Social Democrats were taking their first steps toward a just and egalitarian society in

Sweden. The Republican Roosevelt was the first president to seriously confront the unhealthy, exorbitant accumulations of wealth—and its abuse. Much of his program and ideas were stolen from the populist William Jennings Bryan, but the Democrat Bryan never became president and the Republican Roosevelt did.

Both men warned against amassing of wealth and power in large corporate combinations and in the hands of a few families. Some acquired their wealth in the form of natural resources at low prices from the government by fraud and manipulation.

Roosevelt was president from 1901 to 1909 and established himself as a conservationist and as a "trust buster." After he won a second term in 1904, his attorney general, Philander C. Knox, brought suit under the Sherman Antitrust Act against the Northern Securities Company, which was a holding company of the Great Northern Railway Company, the Northern Pacific and other railroads and J. P. Morgan, the key New York banker. "We do not wish to destroy corporations," Roosevelt said, "but we do wish to make them subserve the public good." The Supreme Court upheld the court action and declared that the holding company was illegal. Altogether, forty-four suits against trusts (corporate combinations) were started during Roosevelt's administration.

In 1912 when he ran again for president as a maverick "Bull Moose" Republican, Roosevelt announced:

> "I stand for the square deal. [Twenty-two years later his cousin, Franklin D. Roosevelt, would proclaim a New Deal.] But when I say that I am for the square deal, I mean not merely that I stand for fair play under the present rules of the game but that *I stand for having those rules changed so as to work for a more substantial equality of opportunity and of reward for equally good service.*" (Emphasis added.)

He didn't win in 1912 because he split the Republicans in two, and the Democratic candidate Woodrow Wilson, another progressive, won handily.

Before World War I dominated the world stage, the Progressive movement, through both Republicans and Democrats, and the action of many enlightened citizens, caused the adoption of the federal income tax; the popular election of U.S. senators (who previously had been elected by state legislators); the creation of the U.S. Department of Commerce and Labor, with a Bureau of Corporations authorized to investigate corporate behavior; the Pure Food and Drug Act, the Federal Reserve Act, and the Clayton Antitrust Act; and the establishment of the Federal Trade Commission.

The Progressive movement in the United States largely passed to the Democrats with the election of Woodrow Wilson in 1912. It gave people what they wanted in stabilizing the capitalist system by repairing some of its worst defects, and it also blunted the edge of the Socialist movement and restored a measure of peace in a time of bitter clashes between capital and labor.

Next came World War I, which no one wanted but the European powers and the United States seemed incapable of avoiding. Eight million died on the battlefield and millions more died of hunger and disease related to the war. It became the most destructive war known up to that time, and brought about the dissolution of the Austro-Hungarian Empire and the creation of new countries and configurations such as Yugoslavia that carried the seeds of future conflict.

On one side there was Germany and the Austro-Hungarian Empire, and on the other side was Britain, France, Russia, and, later, the United States. The conflict started in the Balkans, when the Archduke Ferdinand, heir to the throne of Austria-Hungary, was assassinated in Sarajevo, Bosnia, by a Serbian nationalist in 1914, but soon expanded into the catastrophic war. Most of the fighting occurred in France and Belgium. Britain blockaded German ports and neutral countries near Germany. Germany retaliated with submarines that prowled the North Atlantic and sank ships that might be helping Britain. On May 7, 1915, a British passenger liner, the *Lusitania*, with American passengers and some munitions on board, was torpedoed by a German submarine near the coast of Ireland. This incident was a harbinger of what was to come.

Wilson won a second term in 1916. He was a scholar and idealist, the son of a southern Presbyterian minister. He had been educated at Princeton University, the University of Virginia, and Johns Hopkins University, where he earned a doctorate in political science. Wilson taught at Princeton and in 1902 became its president. He became governor of New Jersey in 1910 and president of the United States in 1913 after winning the November 1912 election.

On a personal note, my dad was unable to go to college, but was a self-made businessman, who voted Republican as long as I knew him, but always considered himself an Independent. When I asked him once why he considered himself an Independent even though he always voted Republican, he said, "I voted for Woodrow Wilson twice." That shut me up.

When the war in Europe started in August 1914, President Wilson immediately issued a proclamation of neutrality, which was supported by the American people, who overwhelmingly opposed going to war even though most of them favored France and Great Britain. In 1917, after Germany stated it would undertake unrestricted submarine warfare and torpedoed and sank six American ships, public opinion turned 180 degrees. Congress passed a war resolution and America entered the conflict.

Always the idealist, Wilson looked beyond the immediate German provocation and in his war message found a higher purpose:

"The World must be made safe for democracy. Its peace must be planted upon the tested foundations of political liberty. We have no selfish ends to serve. We desire no conquest, no dominion. We seek no indemnities for ourselves, no material compensation for the sacrifices we shall freely make. We are but one of the champions of the rights of mankind."

Once America entered the war it went all-out. Congress instituted a draft of all able-bodied men between eighteen and forty-five inclusive. To support the armed forces and the war effort, taxes of all kinds were increased—the highest income tax rates were raised to 63 percent. The country, including all industry and occupations, was put under wartime control, including new restrictions on freedom of the press and speech. By the time the Allies won the war two years later, over two million soldiers had been sent to France and another almost two million more were at home in training for service overseas if needed. One of these soldiers in training was my dad, whom the Army had sent to a technical institute in Minneapolis for training and who would joke that he spent the last year of the war fighting the "Battle of Hennepin Avenue." The armistice came on November 11, 1918. The final peace treaty, signed at Versailles outside Paris, contained the seeds for the later rise of Nazi Germany, but also contained the precursor of the United Nations, the League of Nations, another of Woodrow Wilson's visions that was scuttled when presented to the United States Senate in 1920.

A look at the involvement of the United States and the non-involvement of Sweden in World War I gives us some insight into their more current histories.

As soon as the war started, both countries declared their neutrality. Sweden, which had a long history of participation in European wars and had grown weary of their cost and futility, was determined to stay neutral. Its ports were blockaded by both Britain and Germany, so excuses could have been found to enter the conflict on either side. But by this time Sweden had successfully avoided military conflict for over one hundred years and had learned the benefits of remaining neutral and at peace.

Compared to the older, more mature and cautious Sweden, America was the growing, impetuous, energetic teenager ready to test its strength. Just a few years earlier it had conducted its first war outside its borders: the Spanish-American War had been very successful and drove the "evil" Spanish colonists out of Cuba, Puerto Rico, and the Philippines. The U.S. population was not eagerly looking for war but it was confident and effective when it came. To be charitable, the provocation the United States received was greater than any given to Sweden. The Germans, by the sinking of American ships, quickly became the enemy that had to be punished. America responded and "won" its second war. A pattern had been set for U.S. foreign policy in the twentieth and early twenty-first century: wars and more wars to come.

Another contrast between the two countries that remains today became evident immediately after the war. That is the potential for using an international organization to facilitate the settlement of disputes between sovereign states to help avoid future wars.

Woodrow Wilson engineered the inclusion of such an organization, the League of Nations, into the peace treaty in the form of a covenant that invited all powers to become members. Sweden was one of the first nations to enthusiastically join. The United States, however, was reluctant, and the Senate refused to ratify the plan. Sweden, led by Hjalmar Branting, immediately saw the League providing smaller nations protection from more powerful and aggressive states. U.S. senators, however, immediately saw the League as a threat to their country's sovereignty and freedom of action in the world. Eighty years later this tension between the perspective of the United States under George W. Bush and that of Sweden (along with most other countries in the world) still exists.

After World War I, America disarmed and there was a period of normalcy and prosperity for both countries until the depression of the 1930s. Great leaps forward in industries such as the automobile and aircraft were accomplished. People like Henry Ford and Charles Lindbergh became worldwide icons. The Progressive Era was over in the United States and the so-called Golden Twenties or Jazz Age or Roaring Twenties arrived and were presided over by lackluster Republican presidents Warren G. Harding, Calvin Coolidge, and Herbert Hoover. In Sweden, the engine for change, the Social Democratic Party, was growing, mainly due to universal suffrage, adopted between 1918 and 1920, that removed all restrictions on voting for women and men without property. Greater changes in both Swedish democracy and society were coming but had not yet arrived. There were frequent changes of national leadership in Sweden during this time but no clear-cut decisions on policy.

The shadow of the Great Depression fell over both lands at the end of the 1920s. The crash at the New York Stock Exchange on October 29, 1929, ushered in a wave of bank, private business, and factory closings that, in turn, caused an estimated 12 million men and women in America in 1933 to lose their jobs. In Sweden, increased unemployment brought growing Communist agitation. The economic foundations of both countries were shaken.

By September 1932, the Social Democrats, who had been out of power in Sweden, returned to power through a coalition with the Farmers Party. To provide employment, large public works projects were undertaken, as was done in the United States at the same time and for the same reason. Influenced by the ideas of British economist John Maynard Keynes, the Swedish government continued to spend its way out of the depression. Public expenditures in both countries were regarded as stimuli to the economy and as a way of increasing employment and productivity. On balance, the decade of the 1930s was a period of vibrant economic activity in Sweden, and as a result, it recovered more quickly from the depression than the United States did. Industry was making improvements through efficiencies in using electricity, mechanization, and other scientific improvements, so by 1935, productivity was 20 percent greater than in 1929, with a labor force only 2 percent larger.

The United States undertook similar measures to bring recovery. Franklin D. Roosevelt was elected president in November 1932, the same year the Social Democrats returned to power in Sweden. The major legislative enactments of Roosevelt's New Deal were the National Labor Relations Act and the Social Security Act. He was strongly opposed by the Republicans for reelection in 1936, but proved his popularity by winning all of the states but two: Maine and Vermont. He won an unprecedented third term in 1940.

The term "New Deal" was coined and used by President Roosevelt to describe his administration's establishment of the federal government's responsibility for protecting farmers, workers, and the unemployed, while actively regulating the economy to prevent another serious depression. It is identified with the Democratic Party, but those responsibilities have been historically accepted and extended by both the Democratic and Republican parties from time to time.

In Sweden, politics is quite different because that nation has a parliamentary system that involves a number of different parties, usually six or seven. The United States stands apart from most democracies with only two major parties. For example, the governing party doesn't have to win the majority of votes in Sweden, but must have only a plurality. It then joins with a smaller party or parties to form a ruling coalition government.

In the 1920s and 1930s in Sweden, there continued to be slow but steady progress in social reform. The Social Democrats pushed for fundamental reforms, whereas opposition in the Riksdag took the form of restraining and modifying rather than negating and destroying. The atmosphere was characterized by compromise and consensus, rather than the "winners over losers" atmosphere of American politics.

In Sweden, conservatives who rejected state action found themselves helping to shape programs of social reform; the liberals approved the goals of reforms but not necessarily the methods; the agrarians would trade their support of certain programs for specific gains for farmers; the Communists believed reform too weak and became marginalized. Hence, reforms were enacted gradually, step by step, with compromises and half-measures.

In the 1920s, only minor reforms were accomplished, such as an increase in sickness insurance and a law on arbitration in labor disputes. In the early 1930s, when the Farmers and Social Democrats began working together, there was home building and public works and unemployment insurance and an increase of income tax by 20 percent and inheritance taxes increased on individual heirs. Old-age pensions were expanded in 1935 and 1937, as well as provision for motherhood benefits, marital loans, grants to widows and children, subsidies for school lunches, and twelve-day paid vacations for workers.

In the 1936 election, the big issue the Social Democrats campaigned for was higher pensions for the elderly supported by higher taxes. The Conservative Party wanted more money for national defense and warned against creeping socialism. Seventy-five percent of people voted, and the Conservative seats went from 58 to 44; Social Democrats' seats increased from 104 to 112—still not a majority, but making it by far the largest party and a significant indication of public opinion.

By now there was a readjustment in attitude by the Social Democrats, who had the responsibility of power. Because of the economic crises of the early 1930s, the governing bodies adopted policies more directly in line with people's needs, rather than pursuing political theory. The Marxist principle of *class warfare* was abandoned, replaced with a new program of social equalization and building a happy and cooperative Swedish national community of *folkhemmet*. Thus, there arose a fundamental difference between the contemporary programs of the Social Democrats of Sweden and the New Deal of Franklin D. Roosevelt in the United States. Whereas the Swedish program aimed to transform society for the long run, the American program was designed more to shore up and correct the abuses of the old social structure and help capitalism work better.

During this period there was labor peace in Sweden. Underlying this tranquillity was an understanding—much more likely to happen in a small country—that resolution of labor conflicts was best for the productivity and prosperity of the whole country.

In the two decades from 1919 to 1939, Sweden moved significantly, even if by short steps, on the road to social democracy. The shift began once universal suffrage was established. Having obtained political democracy, the Social Democrats pushed on for more democracy in society itself.

At first the direction was not clear. The fluctuating balance of political parties meant repeated transfers of power. But the Social Democrats increased in popular support and in self-confidence. The rather even division of political opinion then and in future decades tended to check extremism of any kind and to enforce a politics of consensus. The Social Democrats were full of ideas and energy. The other parties did not attempt to block all reforms and changes but considered it their role to critique, moderate, revise, and delay. Thus progress was made in a broad program of social reform, hesitatingly in the 1920s, decisively in the 1930s. But it was not yet the more comprehensive model it was to become.

There remained unresolved issues that would be addressed in the second half of the century, after World War II: nationalization of industries; the possible abolition of the monarchy; disarmament or increased defense spending; reforms in education; elimination of an official state church. Facing the threat of World War II and later the cold war, surprisingly solid national agreement existed on one thing: that Sweden would remain neutral and as independent as possible in foreign affairs.

CHAPTER 8

The United States, 1945–1980:
Hot and Cold Wars

AFTER THE END OF WORLD WAR II, the United States emerged as a major world power, economically and militarily. Fifty years later, at the end of the twentieth century and after the collapse of the Soviet empire, it was to become the world's sole superpower. It has yet to learn the limits of this power and how to use it wisely. This enormous growth came as the United States accepted its role as the only country able and willing to counterbalance Communist Soviet Russia's expanding power throughout the world. It seemed that from 1950 on, the United States was constantly in conflict, starting with the Korean War in 1950, followed by the Vietnam War and the two Gulf Wars, not to mention the overarching cold war with Russia that lasted almost the entire half century.

During this same period, Sweden, keeping a wary eye on the dangerous Russian bear in the neighborhood, maintained its defensive military strength. But with no active wars or military conflicts, it was able to focus on creating as prosperous and egalitarian a society as possible.

World War II and its aftermath brought about an explosion in the growth of America's middle class in the 1950s and beyond. The wartime mobilization of the United States in the 1940s greatly expanded its industrial base, which was financed through a steeply graduated income tax and supported by both liberals and conservatives in Congress and throughout the country. After the war, the so-called GI Bill of Rights and the favorable housing loans made by the Veterans Administration (VA) and the Federal Housing Administration (FHA) enabled millions of Americans to move up into the middle class.

By 1947, some additional 1.2 million veterans overwhelmed colleges and universities, which in 1940 had had a total enrollment of only 1.5 million. Ultimately, 7.8 million veterans were enrolled in some type of G.I. Bill training. The benefits were sufficiently generous to allow hundreds of thousands who had never seriously considered going to college to do so. All tuition was free depending upon the length of time spent in the service, and single veterans received a substance allowance of $65 per month and those who were married received $90 per month—a governmental investment that gave the United States the best-educated workforce in the world at the time. The VA and FHA low-interest housing loans helped transform the United States from a country of mostly renters to one of mostly homeowners.

Almost no one anticipated the country's growth after World War II. The GDP rose to $258 billion in 1948, $285 billion in 1950, $398 billion in 1955, $504 billion in 1960, and $685 billion in 1965.

The political balance between the two major parties, Democrats and Republicans, remained basically the same over the decades of the 1940s, '50s, and '60s, although issues, economic conditions, and facts of war and peace changed. The Democrats were a majority party whose strength lay almost entirely in the South and the big cities. The Republicans were a near-majority party that sometimes elected a president but seldom controlled Congress. Presidential candidates from both parties accepted Roosevelt's New Deal, the Democrats more wholeheartedly than the Republicans, but there were no big antagonistic splits over public policy or foreign affairs. Democrats had strong support from big labor and big-city machines and retained traditional support from white voters in the South.

Republicans received almost unanimous support from big and small business and rolled up big voting percentages in rural areas outside the South. Black voters were traditionally excluded from voting in the South, and conservative white Southerners retained their attachment to the Democratic Party, which had opposed Lincoln and post–Civil War reconstruction by Republicans.

Franklin Roosevelt died early in his fourth term (April 12, 1945), leaving his vice president, Harry Truman, to make the fateful decision to drop the atomic bombs on Japan that brought an end to World War II in August 1945. I remember this period vividly because I had joined the U.S. Navy in June of that year as a senior in high school, but was not inducted until September, after Japan surrendered, assuring myself a peaceful tour of duty in San Diego, California, rather than on a ship supporting the anticipated invasion of Japan.

Immediately after World War II, President Truman and a unified Congress saw the threat of Soviet Russia's expansionist ambitions and countered with aid to Greece and Turkey. Truman promised that "it must be the policy of the United States to support free peoples who are resisting attempted subjugation by armed minorities or by outside pressures." His pronouncement, ever after called the Truman Doctrine, marked the commencement of the cold war that absorbed the United States and the Soviet Union and much of the world for nearly the balance of the twentieth century.

America's fear of world wide Communist expansion started slowly but grew over the ensuing years to engulf its foreign and domestic affairs in the 1950s, '60s, '70s, and '80s. By the 1980s, before the collapse of the Soviet bloc, Russia and America together had hysterically amassed enough atomic bombs and missiles to ensure mutual destruction and to blow up the entire world. Some of this fear was justified by Russia's postwar expansion and domination in Eastern Europe, plus its bellicose pronouncements. However, much was overblown and fueled the disgraceful "Joe McCarthy period" in the 1950s and the tragic Vietnam War in the 1960s and '70s.

A historic achievement for the United States, Western Europe, and the entire world was the implementation of the Marshall Plan, undertaken after World War II. It received its name from Truman's secretary of state, George C. Marshall, who announced it in a speech at the 1947 Harvard University commencement. Most of Europe, especially Germany, was a shambles, and all countries except perhaps Sweden had devastated economies.

In the late 1940s, the United States, with an economy that had grown sharply during the war, was free to expand even further and to help Europe to rebuild. Led by George Marshall and others in the Truman administration and in consultation with Europeans, a remarkable recovery took place in western Germany, France, Great Britain, Denmark, Norway, and the Low Countries. Stalin immediately denounced the plan, thereby excluding eastern Europe, under Soviet occupation or dominance, from this recovery.

It required multilateral cooperation to be successful. European countries had to determine what they needed and the United States would help. Truman appointed a bipartisan committee to develop policy from the American side, and British Foreign Minister Ernest Bevin took the initiative in Europe. Truman asked Congress for $17 billion for a four-year program, and in 1948, an election year, the Republican Congress approved an initial $5 billion. This was more than 2 percent of the United States' gross national product for that year and was later sweepingly described by the *Economist* as "perhaps the greatest example of national generosity in history." Without doubt, the aid and financing the Marshall Plan provided gave a crucial boost to the economies of Western Europe, beginning a period of unparalleled economic growth for both Europe and the United States.

The unanticipated Korean War in 1950 launched America into rearmament and the state of perpetual military preparedness that continues today.

On June 24, 1950, North Korean troops crossed the Thirty-eighth Parallel into South Korea in an apparent attempt to unify the country under Communist rule. Japan had held all of Korea as a colony since the end of the Sino-Japanese War of 1894–95. After the defeat of Japan in 1945, the victorious Allied powers divided Korea in half at the Thirty-eighth Parallel, with the United States dominant in the south and Russia likewise in the north. A Communist government was formed in the north, and both Russia and the United States withdrew their occupying troops. The Republic of Korea was reorganized in the south with Dr. Syngman Rhee as president. When the Communist North invaded, all but 500 American troops had been demobilized, but that was a short-lived situation.

President Truman sought and received an authorization of the United Nations Security Council to send troops to Korea. The U.N. troops were dominated by American forces and commanded by General Douglas MacArthur, who swept north and reached the Chinese border. This prompted China to send in thousands of troops to join with North Korea in driving the U.S. troops south to the capital of Seoul. In February and March of 1951, MacArthur's troops were reinforced and regrouped to mount a counteroffensive that drove the combined Chinese and North Korean forces back to the Thirty-eighth Parallel. After Dwight D. Eisenhower was elected president in 1952, a truce was signed in 1953 creating a demilitarized zone along the Thirty-eighth Parallel. Talks on a permanent settlement of the conflict have continued fruitlessly at Panmunjom ever since. The war was called a U.N. "police action," but it really was another of America's twentieth-century wars. Before it was over, 33,700 American servicemen were killed. Today, over fifty years later, 38,700 U.S. troops remain stationed in South Korea.

American conventional forces had been reduced after the end of World War II on the assumption that the country's monopoly on atomic weapons would deter Communist expansion. It didn't work that way because not all Communist countries (like North Korea and China) automatically followed Russia when their national agendas differed. The United States also was unwilling to use or brandish the bomb when its homeland was not immediately threatened.

Outlays for national defense rose from $13 billion in the fiscal year ending June 1950 to $22 billion in 1951, $44 billion in 1952, and $50 billion in 1953. Congress and the American people followed the lead of Presidents Truman and Eisenhower, and allowed for the setup of the large permanent peacetime military establishment. The United States had never had this before 1950, but has had an extensive military force ever since.

Dwight David Eisenhower, a former commanding general, was elected president in November 1952, and the Republicans won control of both the House and Senate for the first time since 1928. Eisenhower was a political moderate who accepted the Democrats' "New Deal" social legislation and held at bay the more aggressive conservative elements of his own party, those who believed that America had been betrayed by Communists and "fellow travelers" within, and thus "lost" North Korea and Nationalist China to world communism.

In reply to a critical letter from his brother Edgar on domestic policy, Eisenhower wrote, "Should any political party attempt to abolish Social Security, unemployment insurance, and eliminate labor laws and farm programs, you would not hear again of that party in our political history."

Eisenhower, clearly more popular than his party, was given credit by most people for presiding over peace and prosperity in the 1950s. With Democratic congressional support (the Democrats won back the House and Senate in 1954), Eisenhower signed the National Interstate and Defense Highways Act, a public works project of enormous magnitude. He appointed a liberal Republican, former governor of California, Earl Warren, chief justice of the Supreme Court, although years later he considered that act his biggest mistake. He also was a man of balance and deep experience who was prescient enough to warn the country to be wary of the dangers of creating a permanent military-industrial complex—like we have today. In his farewell address to the nation, as he was on the eve of turning the presidential reins over to John Kennedy in 1961, Eisenhower said:

> "This conjunction of an immense military establishment and a large arms industry is new in the American experience. . . . We recognize the imperative need for this development. Yet, we must not fail to comprehend its grave implications. Our toil, resources and livelihood are all involved; so is the very structure of our society.
>
> "In the councils of government, *we must guard against the acquisition of unwarranted influence, whether sought or unsought, by the military-industrial complex. The potential for the disastrous rise of misplaced power exists and will persist.*
>
> "*We must never let the weight of this combination endanger our liberties or democratic processes. . . .*

> Disarmament, with mutual honor and confidence,
> is a continuing imperative. . . ."

Today, more than forty-five years later, the United States spends more on its military "preparedness" than almost all other countries in the world combined.

In 1960, America elected John F. Kennedy, who became its youngest president at forty-two. He defeated Eisenhower's vice president, Richard Nixon, by an eyelash with .3 percent of the popular vote.

In 1960, Kennedy's social programs, such as Medicare, languished in Congress and he turned to foreign affairs. After taking office he approved the Bay of Pigs invasion of Cuba, which had been planned under Eisenhower, but to Kennedy's credit, he publicly accepted full responsibility for what turned out to be a bungled disaster. A year later, he confronted Soviet Russia over the presence of its missiles in Cuba. The world was terrified, but fortunately the missiles were withdrawn and the crisis passed. He visited the Berlin Wall and expressed solidarity with Germans under the Russian gun, but he also set up a Washington-Moscow hotline and signed the Nuclear Test Ban Treaty in 1963. Under Kennedy, several thousand U.S. military personnel went to South Vietnam, but no large escalation had taken place before his death. Through Kennedy and Congress, the United States vastly increased spending for the military and space programs. Kennedy was fatally shot in a motorcade in Dallas, Texas, on November 22, 1963, in the third year of his presidential term. His martyrdom helped realize his legislative legacy under Lyndon Johnson, his vice president.

Kennedy, like Harry Truman before him, had proposed legislation extending financial help for medical costs to seniors already covered by Social Security. This idea had always been opposed by most Republicans and conservative Democrats in Congress because it was to be financed through the Social Security system and had the dreaded appearance of "socialized medicine."

All those living at the time will remember that Kennedy's death was a traumatic event for the whole nation. The aftermath helped Lyndon Johnson win a landslide victory over his conservative opponent, Barry Goldwater, in the 1964 presidential election. Johnson won 61 percent of the vote, the same percentage as Franklin Roosevelt in 1936. He carried hundreds of suburbs and counties that had never voted for a Democratic presidential candidate before. This victory gave Johnson the mandate he needed to pass the historic Medicare legislation and other social legislation that had been stymied in Congress for years.

The Medicare bill passed Congress in July 1965, and President Johnson made a point of flying out to Independence, Missouri, to sign the bill in the presence of the eighty-one-year-old Harry Truman, who had proposed a similar measure nearly twenty years before. Medicare was not and is not universally comprehensive. It applies only to the elderly who are covered by Social Security and pays only some medical costs. However, the enactment of Medicare and the later indexing of Old Age Social Security payments to inflation did much to lessen poverty among America's elderly.

While the Scandinavian countries, Western Europe, and Canada were constructing comprehensive economic security systems for all their citizens, the best the United States could do, distracted by the Vietnam War and the cold war, was provide a ragged, largely local safety net. Even today, over 20 percent of U.S. citizens remain in poverty.

The problem of poverty in America has long been avoided or denied, but not by Lyndon Johnson, who declared a "War on Poverty"

in his first State of the Union Message in 1964. Through his prod-
ding, Congress passed many provisions that became law in August
1964. The War on Poverty programs were different from a large national program of public works directed from Washington, but the
concept was a ground-up economic improvement in local communities through financial assistance. The idea was to identify and attack
local problems.

To encourage and screen initiatives, local community action
boards were to be "democratically" selected by the poor, although
no one was sure how. This initiative was an interesting experience
for me because I served on our local board, which consisted principally of interested citizens and a sprinkling of elected officials.
By this time I had become a practicing lawyer and state representative and served on this board, along with our mayor, as one of
the token elected officials.

The "war on poverty" didn't last, but it did give birth to the Job
Corps, Volunteers in Service to America (VISTA), food stamps,
and Head Start, all programs that have served U.S. society well.

The sixties were a period of growing unrest and awareness by
African American people. One hundred years had passed since
the Civil War and the adoption of the Thirteenth and Fourteenth
amendments to the U.S. Constitution but equal social, economic,
and legal treatment had not yet come to America. The Civil Rights
Act of 1964, passed after John F. Kennedy's death, did much to
integrate public accommodations and workplaces, but the Voting
Rights Act of 1965 brought about the most seismic change. Blacks
in the South had been prevented from voting by various discrimi-
nating devices, and without the vote it was nearly impossible to
influence public officeholders, from their sheriff to their congressional representatives. Dr. Martin Luther King Jr., along with
other black leaders and organizations, showed that nonviolent

protests could be a more powerful weapon if covered by television. Yet King and others also knew that without the power of the vote, blacks could never expect to be treated equally.

In December 1964, Dr. King went to Oslo to accept the Nobel Peace Prize, a prestigious international recognition of his leadership within the civil rights movement. Soon after his return, he decided he would lead nonviolent demonstrations of blacks seeking the right to vote. One such march to the town of Selma, Alabama, erupted in violent arrests by the county sheriff, and a black sharecropper was shot by a state trooper. President Johnson declared that "all Americans should be indignant when one American is denied the right to vote."

The Voting Rights Act was enacted in August 1965. It suspended the operation of literacy tests and other laws restricting voting in any state or county where less than half the voting-age population actually voted. It passed by overwhelming margins and proved to be even more effective than its advocates had predicted. African Americans had entered irrevocably into political life in the South as they had in the North. The new law had enumerable consequences, one of which was that the South shifted from solid Democratic to solid Republican in many future presidential elections.

After Lyndon Johnson's legislative victories in 1964 and 1965, everything started to disintegrate in direct relation to his escalation of the Vietnam War. Both he and Kennedy, and Eisenhower before them, accepted the domino theory that the loss of South Vietnam to the Communist north would trigger further losses in Asia to worldwide communism, especially to the influence of Red China. They never accepted the truth that the Vietnam conflict was essentially a civil war.

As the war escalated and the number of American troops and casualties grew, opposition grew at home and abroad, but Johnson insisted that the United States would never "cut and run." The war

became a disastrous quagmire. Seeing political opposition growing in his own party, and after almost losing the New Hampshire
primary to Senator Eugene McCarthy of Minnesota, Johnson
announced that he would not be a candidate for reelection in
1968. After a tumultuous convention in Chicago in July 1968, the
Democrats chose Hubert Humphrey, Johnson's vice president, as
their nominee. He was then defeated in the general election by
Richard Nixon, who had emerged from political wilderness to become the Republican nominee. Throughout the campaign, Nixon
maintained that he had a secret plan to reach "peace with honor."
After additional fighting and U.S. bombing of North Vietnam
and neighboring Cambodia, the Americans withdrew from South
Vietnam and signed a peace treaty in Paris in 1973 that essentially
united the country under the Communists. The Vietnam War se-
verely divided the United States and cost 47,350 American lives
and an estimated two million Vietnamese lives.

Richard Nixon was an insecure, paranoid man who had lists
of "enemies" and whose reelection committee sent "hired hands"
to break into the offices of Democratic National Committee in
Washington, D.C., with the goal of planting electronic bugs. The
cover-up of this comical escapade by Nixon and his associates was
exposed by the *Washington Post,* led to his near impeachment, and
caused his resignation in August 1975, elevating Gerald Ford to the
presidency. Ford, after becoming president, pardoned Nixon for
any crimes committed, and this act more than anything else caused
him to be defeated for the presidency by Jimmy Carter in 1976.

Nixon was a paradox. Raised as a Quaker, he solidified his early
political career as a conservative anti-Communist congressman
from California. Then he served as Dwight Eisenhower's vice president, but Eisenhower never liked or trusted him. He lost his first
presidential run to a more telegenic, charismatic John F. Kennedy,
and then promptly lost an attempt to be elected governor of Cali-

fornia. After that defeat, he told the press that they "wouldn't have Richard Nixon to kick around anymore." Nevertheless, ten years later, he achieved his goal and was elected president in the midst of the Vietnam War, which for some took too long to end and for others ended too soon. But, Nixon opened the door to relations with Communist China, a step that only a Republican president with anti-Communist credentials could politically take. He championed and instituted many liberal initiatives, including greater sharing of federal income taxes with the states. He also took positive steps in fighting pollution by setting up the federal Environmental Protection Agency. He also proposed minimum federal payments to needy families with children and a form of national health insurance, neither of which was enacted.

During the Johnson-Nixon period (and both before and beyond, actually), nothing was more dangerous in politics than to be seen as "soft on communism" or "not supporting our troops in the Vietnam War." Running counter to this was the argument that although the United States was the greatest nation in the world with the greatest freedoms and opportunities, it had no business trying to become the world's "policeman."

Neither the presidencies of Lyndon Johnson nor Richard Nixon could successfully reconcile these inconsistencies, and most Americans were left angry and alienated from their political leaders and their government. There was no consensus or focus remaining to build what Lyndon Johnson had named "A Great Society" and little confidence in the country's basic institutions. By covering up the Watergate scandal, President Nixon lost the confidence of the American people and resigned before impeachment and removal from office.

Jimmy Carter, a graduate of the U.S. Naval Academy, a former governor of Georgia, and a peanut farmer, ran and won against Gerald Ford as "a breath of fresh air." He also ran as an outsider unconnected to the Washington, D.C. political establishment. He signed the Panama Treaty, which ceded the ownership of the Panama Canal back to Panama and he resumed diplomatic relations with China. During his presidency, the shah of Iran fled to the United States, which prompted Iranian militants to seize the U.S. Embassy in Tehran and demand that the shah come back in return for a release of U.S. hostages. At the same time, inflation reached new highs as OPEC doubled the price of oil. Between the so-called Hostage Crisis and record-setting inflation, the stage was set for Carter's defeat in 1980.

CHAPTER 9

The New Swedish Model, 1945 to the Present

I WENT TO SWEDEN for the first time in 1949, when I was twenty years old. As a junior in college, I took the summer to tour Europe on the cheap with two friends, Jack Powers and Neil Franey. It was a life-changing event for me. We crossed the Atlantic with a thousand other American students in a Dutch passenger liner that had been converted to a troop ship during the war. Our "educational" package cost $325 and gave us passage to Rotterdam in late June and train fare to Paris with ten days' lodging on the Left Bank. After that we were on our own until we returned to the same ship in Rotterdam in late August for passage back to New York in time for fall semester in September. The three of us, after our stay in Paris, took the train to Nice and Monte Carlo on the Riviera and later hitchhiked and rode the train into Italy, Switzerland, and Bavaria in southern Germany. Next we traveled north by train through Germany to Denmark. This was just when the Marshall Plan for rebuilding Western Europe was beginning. The extensive bombing damage we saw in Frankfurt and other German cities was horrendous and unforgettable.

From Copenhagen, Denmark, the three of us went on to Stockholm, Sweden. Neil decided to spend the balance of his time in Germany and the Netherlands before returning to our ship in Rotterdam. Jack and I hitchhiked in Sweden to the city of Karlstad near the Norwegian border, and there we split. He went on to Norway to see its magnificent fjords, and I hitched a ride about thirty miles farther to the village of Eksharad, in Värmland, where I was welcomed by relatives who remembered my grandparents on my mother's side (mormor and morfar). Spending over a week in this beautiful forest highland countryside was like an ascension to paradise after our exhausting trip through Europe. I spoke only a few Swedish words but soon learned that most young people had taken five or six years of English in school and enjoyed practicing their skills on an American.

It wasn't until years later that I realized that my first visit to Sweden in 1949 came at such a watershed in the history of the two countries. Sweden was on the cusp of taking its turn to the left in forming a society that would embrace more equality and close the gap between rich and poor. The United States was completing its disarmament from World War II but was soon to rearm to fight hot and cold wars and become more nationalistic and conservative and eventually increase the gap between rich and poor. (More about that later.)

The so-called Swedish Model is generally associated with minimal poverty, surprising equality, a high level of employment among women and men, and the greater likelihood of a similar lifestyle for all. In other words, the Swedish people created a huge middle class. The model wasn't adopted overnight, nor has it remained static. The roots of democratic collective action, coupled with ethical and religious concern for the poor, run deep in Swedish tradition. Only in recent centuries, however, have the special privileges of the crown, the nobles, and the clergy been eroded. A historical class system was replaced by a meritocracy similar to what we have in the United States but without leaving a large group in poverty. The political, ideological, and economic conditions necessary for the creation of the modern Swedish welfare state came together only after 1945.

The Great Depression of the 1930s caused Sweden, like the United States, to search for a system that would keep its people from ever again having to suffer from humiliating poverty. In the United States, President Franklin Roosevelt and his Democratic New Deal initiated a host of temporary programs of public works and more permanent regulation of business and finance. The most significant attempt to create a "safety net" for workers and their families in the United States was the Social Security system adopted in 1935.

In Sweden, the Social Democratic Party, in coalition with other political parties, particularly the Farmer Party, led the way in building the *folkhemmet,* or "people's home," starting with unemployment benefits in 1934. Through extensive planning, discussion, and consensus building, the so-called Swedish Model was created after 1945 and now provides the following benefits:

- Free public education from preschool through university
- Comprehensive universal health care
- National child allowance
- Unemployment benefits of about 80 percent of former earnings
- Job retraining and relocation
- Subsidized day care
- Housing allowances for families with children
- Paid parental leaves up to sixteen months to care for newborn children
- Regular and supplementary retirement pensions
- Guaranteed five-week paid vacations
- Low-cost public transportation
- Subsidized art and cultural programs

These programs were created slowly and only after in-depth study by parliamentary commissions that included experts in the various fields, politicians and representatives of interest groups such as workers and employers. Folkhemmet grew when the economy flourished in the 1950s, '60s, and '70s and money was available to fund these programs. Although Sweden's boom was not particularly unique, it was important that a consensus was built by the government together with labor and business to take advantage of this growth to establish a strong framework for a more productive and equal society. There was no economic drain caused by wars or arms races that would have made these public benefits much more difficult to finance.

In the field of social welfare, Sweden (and the other Nordic countries of Norway, Denmark, Finland, and Iceland) now represent a universal model in which all citizens are given a range of publicly subsidized services, from child care to elder care, from "cradle to grave." The Swedish Model was often labeled "The Middle Way" between communism and democratic capitalism. This term is misleading because Sweden never was close to Russian communism with its totalitarian one-party government and state-owned industries. It has long been highly democratic with a multiparty parliamentary system and active citizen participation. There were never any successful attempts to seize and nationalize industries. Success has been achieved through a high degree of consensus and cooperation between labor and management, but that has not eliminated all underlying conflicts between interest groups. It would be wrong to claim that the Swedish social welfare model is perfect. By any measure, however, it has worked very well for decades and has been changed and adjusted through peaceful democratic methods.

Any description of the creation of the modern Swedish state must recognize the leadership of the Social Democratic Party.

Hjalmar Branting was its early leader and an occasional prime minister in the 1920s. He was followed by Per Albin Hansson, who was prime minister from 1932 to 1946, roughly the same period that Franklin Roosevelt was president of the United States. Hansson, originally a journalist, was a leading figure in the development of the concept of the folkhemmet and the legislative program leading to its eventual enactment. During World War II, he led the wartime coalition government through difficult times. He died suddenly in 1946 and was succeeded by another Social Democrat, Tage Erlander, who was prime minister for twenty-three years during the successful adoption of the Swedish folkhemmet we know today. He, in my opinion, is largely the unsung hero of the movement. A tall, lanky man, he was an astute and able politician whose personal and nonconfrontational style allowed him to build the essential coalitions that brought about the consensus so essential in a productive parliamentary system.

Olof Palme, a much more dynamic and controversial figure, became the Social Democrat leader in 1969, when Erlander retired. Palme served as prime minister until 1976, when the Social Democrats temporarily lost power, but returned to office in 1982. He was very outspoken in foreign affairs and voiced his opposition to the United States' war in Vietnam. No one in Sweden thought of the job of prime minister as particularly risky and needing ever present bodyguards, so it shocked the nation when Palme was assassinated in 1986 as he and his wife were walking home alone after seeing a movie in downtown Stockholm. The crime remains unsolved, although a suspect was arrested and released. No apparent political motive in the killing has ever been established.

Elements that made Sweden an ideal place to create a more egalitarian state during the 1950s and '60s was Western prosperity, of course, and the blurring of historic class lines that had already occurred. Meritocracy had largely replaced an aristocracy of landed nobles and powerful clergy. Through established political parties, elements of society were represented in the modern parliamentary democracy, and there was an educated, engaged electorate, open to pragmatic change and free of a deeply ingrained suspicion of any governmental action.

This new model drew on the ancient precedents of cooperation and collective action in the early close-knit peasant communities and in the Christian parishes of the Middle Ages that cared for the weak. The idea of *jämlikhet* (equality) also had ancient roots and became a popular slogan of this movement toward a new societal model. The concept called for the elimination of privileged social classes, particularly in education, and the establishment of true social and wage solidarity. It opposed the concentration of privilege and power groups favored by tradition but rather sought to give all people an underpinning of financial security and equality. A majority of Swedes believed that every citizen was entitled to a moderate level of financial security and opportunity. Taxation to support this kind of society was understood and accepted. Opposition to any governmental action does not run as deep in Sweden as it does in the United States.

Steven Koblik, a perceptive historian and commentator on Swedish society, wrote in 1988 about the moral values that underpin modern Sweden:

> The church's influence in providing moral guidance seems to have been on the wane since the late nineteenth century. The free churches were more dynamic than the state church and integrated into other "people's movements" (unions, cooperatives, prohibition, Liberal and Social Democratic parties) that were instrumental in modernizing the country. The moral tenets of Christianity became integral elements within these groups and have been

sustained in the welfare state. One need only to read the popular press, listen to political debate, or examine primary and secondary curricula to recognize that Christian values are firmly entrenched in the society. Granted these values do not include what most Americans think of as Christian attitudes toward sex, and most younger Swedes probably do not realize that the value system they received from parents and social institutions is religiously based. (p. 604 in Scott)

While the United States fought against communism during the Vietnam War and the cold war, Sweden, along with other countries in Western Europe, democratically increased public spending and taxation, thus creating prosperous and more equal societies. This shift was not accomplished instantly and will always remain a work in progress. However, because much has been archieved and has now been tested for several generations, *a reasonable conclusion can be drawn: namely, that large increases in public spending and taxation, democratically adopted and intelligently planned to benefit all citizens, do not deter a country's economic growth.*

Peter H. Lindert's *Growing Public: Social Spending and Economic Growth since the Eighteenth Century,* a comprehensive study of the social spending of nineteen countries and its effect on their economic growth, was published in 2004. A distinguished economic historian and professor at the University of California, Davis, Lindert convincingly refutes the notion that increased public spending on programs such as health, education, pensions, and child care will dampen a country's economic growth. In fact, such spending, if wise, can enhance growth, and the taxes public programs require do not adversely affect business enterprise and necessary capital formation. What was particularly fascinating to me was his examination of the experience of the Swedish welfare state during recent decades. Lindert determined that "core social programs did not malfunction, nor did they shrink or become unpopular."

What has been created in Sweden over the past fifty years is contrary to the conventional wisdom held by many academic and conservative economists, who rely principally on their theoretical models. In the real world, Sweden has had a functioning democracy in which 80 percent of citizens vote and the political parties work together to form a consensus that has protected all of the people, including the business and entrepreneurial sector, while raising taxes on everyone, including high consumption taxes. On the spending side there has been investment in education, health care, and child care that encouraged workers' productivity and employment. This is especially true among women in Sweden, who are employed in greater numbers and earn pay closer to that of men than in any other country in the world.

The familiar mantra of conservatives in the United States is that tax cuts for the wealthy and reductions in public services (except the military, of course) will always stimulate economic growth. Sweden has done just the opposite and has done quite well. Sweden's growth in gross domestic product (GDP) was 4.4 percent in 2006, higher than the United States and any other European country. Remember, however, that in evaluating the morality of any society, how it distributes its wealth is always more important that its GDP.

The last half-century was one of the most dynamic in all of Sweden's long history. A culture of consensus-based democracy has been firmly established. Sweden is environmentally beautiful and clean, intellectually and culturally stimulating, egalitarian, and prosperous. Dissenting and critical views are openly advanced and discussed in the media and during political campaigns. A minority of residents believe that change has gone too far and is too costly and that a stifling uniformity has been created. Conservative parties espousing this view have for short periods held the prime minister-ship, but the Social Democrats have always been returned to office.

At the beginning of the twenty-first century, the Swedish economy is in good shape. The central government has budget and trade surpluses, inflation is low, growth is healthy, and un-employment is falling. In the 2002 election, the Social Democrats received a plurality and formed a coalition government with two small left-leaning parties. The national election in 2006 shifted from center-left to center-right.

In today's global market, Sweden has the ability to compete in knowledge-based sectors such as information technology, tele-communications, and biotechnology because of its highly skilled workforce and flair for innovation. The World Economic Forum, a Geneva-based think tank, ranked Sweden's economy as the third most competitive in the world in 2002.

Despite Sweden's many achievements, I've never met any Swedes who said their country was the "best" or the "greatest." They don't talk that way. But I also have never met a Swede who, when asked, didn't say that he or she loved Sweden.

CHAPTER 10

The United States, Moving into the Twenty-First Century: Reagan, Bush I, Clinton, and Bush II

I N NOVEMBER 1980, Ronald Reagan defeated the Democratic incumbent, Jimmy Carter, for president. His election was the watershed that facilitated the rise and eventual political dominance of the Republican Right in America. Immediately after he was sworn in, Iran released the fifty-two American hostages it had been holding during the last months of Carter's presidency. During the campaign, the televised presidential debates were pivotal. The challenger, Reagan, a practiced communicator, was able to change his impression from that of a mediocre Hollywood actor to that of a credible potential president. The campaign showed that Reagan was a masterful political opponent with genuine down-home charismatic appeal. The pollsters predicted a close election, but Reagan, who promised to get the government "off the backs of the American people," was able to reach conservatives across party lines and carried forty-four states with a total of 489 electoral votes out of 538. The Republicans also picked up twelve seats in the Senate (giving them a majority for the first time in twenty-five years) and thirty-three seats in the House. We still have a coffee cup I gave to my wife that reads "Democrat

1980" with a picture of a donkey. I gave it in jest, saying that we might become the last of a breed and that the mug could become a historical artifact.

Jimmy Carter left the White House largely discredited, but his personal reputation has grown substantially since. As an ex-president, he has been a prolific writer and has won universal recognition and affection as a humanitarian and as a trustworthy international mediator. (Maybe he's part Swedish.) He was awarded the Nobel Peace Prize in 2002 "for his decades of untiring effort to find peaceful solutions to international conflicts, to advance democracy and human rights, and to promote economic and social development."

Ronald Reagan was a unique political character and even today not easily understood. When he first arrived in Washington as president, he was described by some in the Democratic establishment as an "amiable dunce." That perception has not been completely erased, but after serving eight years during the end of the cold war and since his death in 2004, he is more often recognized as a gifted and complex leader who has become the icon of the modern conservative movement in America and a patron saint of the Republican Party, in contrast to Richard Nixon, who's seldom mentioned any more in proper Republican circles.

I remember listening to Reagan's acceptance speech at the Republican convention in 1980 on the car radio and thinking to myself, This dude should be easy to defeat. He promised to cut domestic spending and substantially increase military spending while greatly cutting federal taxes and balancing the budget—all at the same time. I thought, Good, Nobody will believe that! (During the preconvention Republican primaries, running-mate-to-be George H. W. Bush had labeled Reagan's ideas "voodoo economics.") I was wrong. Most voters must have believed the promises or ignored them. Meanwhile, Bush recanted his "voodoo" description during the campaign.

The first thing Reagan did after his nomination is something that remains unforgivable to me, even today. He immediately launched his presidential campaign in Philadelphia, Mississippi, where three civil rights volunteers working to register black voters had been murdered. His speech extolled states' rights, letting all white Southerners know he was on "their side." Everyone, especially Southerners, black and white, knew that "states' rights" in that context was the code word for discrimination against African Americans.

The presidency of Ronald Reagan was in some ways an enigma. He was a smaller-government conservative who tripled the national debt. When younger, he was a Democrat who admired Franklin Roosevelt and always voted for him. He also had been an officer of the Screen Actors Guild in Hollywood, but as president, he pulverized organized labor by firing more than ten thousand members of the air traffic controllers union. He paid lip service to the agenda of the Christian Right but was a divorced man, the first president to invite a gay couple to stay at the White House, and signed one of the most liberal state abortion laws when he was governor of California. He was successful in keeping the extreme religious conservatives at bay. He considered Communist Russia the "Evil Empire," but on a personal level, he liked and trusted Mikhail Gorbachev so much that together they were able to hasten the end of the cold war. Reagan angered many who saw him as indifferent to the victims of HIV/AIDS, callous to the plight of the poor, and a promoter of the stereotype of the fraudulent "welfare queen" who drove a Cadillac. But he charmed most people with his sunny disposition and self-deprecating humor. He joked about his work habits and said, "It's true hard work never killed anybody, but I figure why take the chance." The news media liked him, and he became known as the "Teflon President" because criticism never stuck to him.

Most important, Reagan has been given credit by many for ending the cold war. The inefficiencies of a Communist one-party command economy made the disintegration of the Russian empire inevitable, and the breakup of the Soviet bloc had already begun when Reagan came to office. However, he undoubtedly hastened its demise by convincing the United States and its European allies that a large increase in nuclear arms and the deployment of rocket missiles would cause an eventual elimination of the Soviet threat. Reagan wanted to go beyond the policy of containment, although it had successfully avoided any direct war with the Soviet Union for years. He pushed rhetorically for the rollback of the "evil empire," but fortunately for the world and its inhabitants, this dismantling was accomplished without a nuclear war. Much of the credit for ending the cold war must also be given to the realism and leadership of Reagan's negotiation partner, the Soviet Union's president Mikhail Gorbachev, who knew that his country could no longer sustain an expensive escalating arms race and contain its restive members (Latvia, Estonia, Lithuania, Ukraine, etc.).

In 1985 and 1986, Reagan had his first and second summit meetings with Gorbachev, which established trust between the two leaders. In 1987, their third summit produced an agreement to dismantle the medium-range missiles in Europe, marking the beginning of the end of the cold war.

None of this could have been accomplished without financial cost. America's military spending was increased by a third during Reagan's first term while he pushed through tax cuts that resulted in the largest deficits in American history up to that time and tripled the national debt. The economy grew and the Republican Party changed from its historical role as the party of fiscal conservatism to the party of spending and borrowing. Twenty years later, this pattern has been repeated by the George W. Bush administration, beginning in 2000. Vice President Dick Cheney asserted that "Ronald Reagan proved that deficits don't matter." (For a contrary, more realistic view, I strongly recommend the recent excellent book *Running on Empty* by Peter G. Peterson, former Republican secretary of commerce under Richard Nixon.)

Throughout his presidency, Reagan was a personable, charismatic, optimistic leader. It wasn't until the so-called Iran-contra scandal at the end of his second term that his popularity temporarily waned. However, he was given a free pass by the American people, who attributed his nearly complete disengagement and lack of responsibility to his advanced age and loose management style.

Later, after leaving office, some of his White House staff were prosecuted and convicted of illegally trading arms for hostages and secretly diverting monies to rebels in Nicaragua whom Reagan supported. When they came to trial in 1990, the former president testified about his role and responded to questions 130 times with "I don't recall" or "I don't remember." Then, in 1995, he revealed publicly that he was suffering from Alzheimer's disease.

Ronald Reagan was one of the most consequential presidents of the twentieth century because he came along and caught a conservative wave that was in its ascendance. He was able to articulate its core beliefs and give it a currency that took it through the next twenty-five years. After the unrest and conflict of the 1960s and '70s, with the assassinations of John and Robert Kennedy and Martin Luther King, and the painful, divisive war in Vietnam, the country was ready for Reagan's optimistic vision that America was still the last best hope of humankind and had a mission to triumph over the Soviet Union. He told us it was "morning in America." He remained undeterred in seeing problems in simple terms of good and evil, right and wrong. He was able to tap into the belief of many Americans that we are exceptional and chosen by God to spread our ideal democracy to the rest of the world.

When Reagan arrived on the scene, the obstacle that stood in

America's way was the Soviet Union. It had to be removed, not to be punished or dominated, but to allow for the completion of our mission, akin to that of Woodrow Wilson, "to make the world safe for democracy."

Other ideas and beliefs Reagan held may not have been as visionary, but he gave voice to them and allowed them to become part of the fabric of the conservative agenda. One idea was to delegitimize any federal action, except the military. That notion requires the search for a private business solution to any public problem because a profit motive makes people act more efficiently. A good example is America's aversion to anything called "socialized medicine," as they have in Sweden, even though the most efficient half of our health care system is already socialized in Medicare and the Veterans Administration. Another belief is that tax cuts for the wealthy are good for everyone because these cuts encourage capital accumulation for the wealthy, who then invest their money in businesses that create jobs that spur the economy with the resulting wealth trickling down to the poor. Another belief strengthened by Reagan and largely adopted by both major parties in the United States is that military spending has priority over domestic spending, and any hesitation about "projecting our power" in the world is a sign of weakness, if not downright unpatriotic.

These core conservative beliefs did not originate with Reagan, but he gave them an articulate voice that has taken hold and been advanced by the current Bush administration.

After eight years, Ronald Reagan bequeathed the presidency and his leadership of the Conservative Revolution to his vice president, George H. W. Bush, who lost everything within four short years to two young political animals. The leadership of the Republican conservatives he lost to Congressman Newt Gingrich (R-GA), and the presidency was surrendered after one term to Arkansas governor Bill Clinton and the Democrats.

The presidential election of 1988 was between two lackluster candidates, the Republican Vice President Bush and Democrat Michael Dukakis, governor of Massachusetts. Bush had emerged unscathed by the Reagan White House's Iran-contra scandal. He vowed to follow the popular Reagan's legacy of less government, a strong military, "family values," and no new taxes. In addition, Bush ran the type of scurrilous campaign that "defines" a presidential opponent in starkly negative terms through television and surrogates. Dukakis, by clear implication, was held responsible in television ads for the murder of a woman by a scary-looking African American rapist who was released from prison on a weekend furlough under a law passed by the Massachusetts legislature and signed by Dukakis. Bush also "accused" Dukakis of being a "card-carrying member" of the reputable, independent American Civil Liberties Union, which takes legal action supporting people's civil liberties regardless of their status or politics. Those of us over sixty remember a time when Joe McCarthy liked to use the epithet "card-carrying member of the Communist Party" to destroy his enemies.

Vivid in my memory of the Bush-Dukakis election campaign was what my sister Carol, a liberal Democrat from Massachusetts, encountered when she visited her hometown in Minnesota in the fall of 1988. She went to a dinner party with old friends and a number of other couples. Most of them were upper-middle-class business and professional people similar to Carol, a school teacher married to a professor at Wellesley College. Not surprisingly, she favored Michael Dukakis, who, in her opinion, had been a fine, honest governor and would make an excellent president. She told me shortly after the dinner how shocked she was by the intense negative opinions most everyone had of Dukakis as a dangerous, liberal, incompetent, evil man. The aristocratic George H. W. Bush had already effectively sold himself as a defender of all-American values against the dangerous Harvard Yard liberalism of Michael Dukakis.

Dukakis led Bush in the early opinion polls in the spring, but as Bush started to run as a conservative redneck against a New England liberal, the old Reagan coalition rallied behind him and he won the popular vote by 53 percent, the Evangelical Christian vote by 81 percent, and a majority of white males at all income levels.

Although Bush had impeccable Republican credentials, having loyally served with Ronald Reagan for eight years and earlier having been the chairman of the national Republican Party, he was never really accepted and trusted by the right wing of his own party. This may have been because his father, Prescott Bush, had been a moderate Republican senator from Connecticut, or it might have been simply because he wasn't Ronald Reagan. When he said he sought a "kinder, gentler" nation and wanted to be known as the "environmental president," many conservatives grumbled that he was echoing liberal slander about Reagan. What proved to be his most damaging campaign promise was, "Read my lips: no new taxes."

In the second year of his presidency, Bush became convinced that the only way to get the economy back in shape after the large Reagan deficits was to increase revenue by raising taxes. He negotiated a deficit reform package with the Democratic congressional leadership that included some new taxes and assumed he would be supported by most Republicans. Congressman Newt Gingrich rallied rebellious conservative troops to vote against the president's bill, and with Democratic help it was defeated. Bush felt the only way to save face and responsibly control growing deficits was to lure additional liberal Democratic votes. This was accomplished by a new bill that raised the top income tax rates from

28 percent to 31 percent and was passed with Democratic votes and signed by the President. Many conservatives in and out of Congress regarded Bush as a traitor for breaking his pledge not to raise taxes.

In late 1990, Saddam Hussein suddenly invaded his southern neighbor, Kuwait, and 200,000 U.S. troops were immediately moved to Saudi Arabia in response. In early 1991, President Bush ordered the commencement of the Desert Storm War that lasted five days and pushed Iraq out of Kuwait. Coalition troops (mainly American) drove deep into Iraq itself but stopped short of Baghdad because Bush knew that Iraq's military had been effectively destroyed. He also knew that he had not planned an exit strategy if Saddam were toppled. He and others believed that Americans were not prepared for the long-term occupation and rebuilding of Iraq that would be required.

For the most part, the American people agreed with Bush's wise decision to stop and withdraw, and his popularity soared in early 1991 to stratospheric heights. During this time, members of his team included Colin Powell, chairman of the Joint Chiefs of Staff, and Dick Cheney, secretary of defense. Familiar names. Later, some critics question whether Bush ordered a cease-fire too early, which allowed Saddam Hussein to retain his despotic power in Iraq. This decision, some believe, may have been one of the unstated reasons why his son, George W. Bush, started a war in 2003, with the goal of regime change in Iraq. This remains pure speculation. All we know is that the stated reason for the invasion of Iraq, to find and eliminate weapons of mass destruction, was not true.

How the first President Bush lost the election of 1992 to Bill Clinton when he was so extremely popular a year earlier is hard for me to explain. One big element has to have been the unique

American electoral system, which allows a third-party candidate who can't win the presidency himself, to effectively choose the winner. Enter Ross Perot. With his millions of dollars and novel, quirky personality, Perot was able to create a national Independent Party (basically Libertarian) that many found attractive. He won 19 percent of the popular vote but no electoral votes. However, he drew more votes away from Republican Bush than from Democrat Clinton, thus giving Clinton the victory. This was the best showing of a third-party candidate since 1912 when Teddy Roosevelt ran and lost as a Bull Moose Party candidate and split the Republican base, thus electing the Democrat, Woodrow Wilson.

Just as George H. W. Bush underestimated Bill Clinton, Clinton, in turn, overestimated the mandate he had received from the American electorate. He and his wife, Hillary, failed miserably when they immediately attempted to craft universal health care legislation that could pass Congress. However, after a rocky start, Clinton gained a firmer footing and won a standoff against House Speaker Newt Gingrich over a government shutdown caused by a budget impasse. With the stock market soaring, unemployment falling, and inflation in check, Clinton defeated the dour Bob Dole almost effortlessly for a second term. Clinton presided over prosperous business years when he governed as a centrist in his second term with no big new liberal programs. However, with Republican help, he passed welfare reform into law. Millions of new jobs were created during the 1990s, and the budget deficit became a surplus through the Clinton administration's fiscal discipline. He left the country with eight years of peace and prosperity and even paid a small amount on the national debt.

Although Clinton was and is an extremely intelligent and knowledgeable man with an empathetic touch that endeared him to millions, he also was seen as the devil incarnate by some who felt that he was an unprincipled, slippery politician who had no right to be president. Throughout his tenure he was investigated by a special prosecutor with unlimited funds provided by Congress. The investigation of an Arkansas land deal the Clintons were involved in came to naught, but it morphed into the investigation of a sexual affair Clinton stupidly had with a White House intern, Monica Lewinsky. When he lied under oath in a deposition in a civil case about this affair it grew into a major public scandal that led to his impeachment (indictment) by the Republican House, followed by a trial in the Republican Senate, where the charges were dismissed. It provided months of entertainment and titillation for the world public and an unavoidable footnote for the history of Clinton's presidency.

Throughout the 1990s, the conservative Reagan wing of the Republican Party continued to grow and strengthen, even though Bill Clinton, a Democrat, was president for eight of these ten years. The expansion of conservative talk radio during this period was phenomenal. Pundits are now heard over six hundred stations around the country. Conservative think tanks and magazines expanded and produced material for writers and commentators that spread their message. This trend provided a continuous drumbeat attacking liberals and President Clinton in particular, and Democrats in general even when there was no election pending. The Republican sound machine relentlessly maligned the mainstream media as if Republicans were the outsiders and somehow the victims of "liberals" even though they controlled all branches of government and a sizable part of TV news.

During my lifetime, the presidential elections have moved from an every-fourth-year event to a perpetual round of fund-raising and political appearances controlled by the White House. This practice began to some degree when the telegenic John F. Kennedy became president. It was perfected by the genial Ronald Reagan in the 1980s. And it became perpetual with Bill Clinton and, then, George W. Bush, who started flying around the country constantly holding fund-raisers and campaigning (to use Hunter Thompson's description of Hubert Humphrey, "like a rat in heat") months before anyone even knew who his Democratic opponent might be.

When George W. Bush was elected in 2000 (even though he was the runner-up in the popular vote), hard-core, black belt conservatives saw in him the leader who would help them achieve their vision of smaller government, lower taxes on wealth accumulation, and a dismantled Social Security. Their crusade had been a long one. I can remember proudly wearing a Kansas sunflower campaign button for Governor Alf Landon to elementary school in 1936 when most of the other kids had FDR buttons. Since that time, I've learned that the Republican Landon maintained that the promise of secure retirement support under Social Security was a "hoax." Obviously, Social Security has been a target of conservative Republicans since its inception.

In addition to the smaller government crowd, the so-called neoconservative wing of the Republican Party has pushed its determination that the United States should step forward in world leadership and against rogue nations by using its unquestioned military dominance more aggressively with less dependence on the United Nations and traditional European allies.

Most Americans were unaware of the neocons' long-term conservative agenda and its implications. They didn't see it coming, because Bush campaigned as a "compassionate conservative" (his term) who in foreign affairs was against "nation building" and, like Teddy Roosevelt, would "walk softly and carry a big stick." They saw a plain-talking Christian conservative who would govern conservatively, hold down taxes, and restore dignity and respect to the White House.

How will this conservative Republican agenda of no new taxes, starving the beast of government, building a new nation in Iraq, and spreading our form of democracy around the world be accomplished? We don't know yet.

We do know that the invasion and occupation of Iraq has been far bloodier and more expensive than expected. We also know that taxes will not be raised to pay for our obligations as long as the country can keep on borrowing money. The annual budget deficit ballooned in the first term of the current Bush administration. It went from the modest surplus he inherited from Clinton to a huge deficit of over $400 billion, causing the total debt to jump from $5.7 trillion in 2000 to over $8 trillion in 2005—far and away the highest national debt in the country's history. At the same time, projected entitlements have been increased for new Medicare drug benefits while federal income was decreased through tax cuts, mainly for the wealthy, leaving a dangerous fiscal mess.

The person selected to lead the American people into accepting this Republican vision of preemptive war and skyrocketing debt is George Walker Bush. After six years as governor of Texas, he became president. Prior to that he led the life of a sociable, wealthy young man from a privileged background who hadn't accomplished much on his own. But he was a likable guy who loved the family business—politics—and there he excelled once he dropped his partying ways. He is an effective salesman and a risk taker, not limited by any uncertainty or regrets. Those members of the Bush cabinet who have questioned the wisdom of some of his important fiscal and military decisions, Colin Powell, secretary of state, and Paul O'Neill, treasury secretary, left the cabinet. So the president was surrounded by a cabinet and a White House staff that provide support and spin for his every public move and statement.

After President Bush won the close reelection over Democrat

John Kerry in 2004 his administration started to seriously unravel. His attempt to privatize Social Security went nowhere. The occupation of Iraq went from bad to worse. The 2006 congressional elections may have marked an end to the total domination by the conservative right in American politics. In the words of President Bush he took a "thumpin'" when the voters changed the leadership in both House and Senate to the Democrats.

The presidential and congressional elections in 2008 should clarify the country's future course.

PART TWO

Contrasting Sweden
and the United States Today

"Move to Sweden."

CHAPTER II

Democratic Governance

To UNDERSTAND DIFFERENCES in how the government is run in Sweden and in the United States, it helps to remember how the two systems evolved. Today they are both modern democracies with free market economies, guaranteed freedoms of expression, and dedicated to the rule of law.

Both countries have a long history of democratic decision making at the community level. In Sweden the tradition goes back to the Vikings, and in America it was practiced in the colonies for generations long before they became the states that united to form a federal government under one constitution. Universal voting took a long time to achieve in both countries, where property and gender requirements had to be met to be eligible to vote and hold office. The most egregious restrictions were applied in the United States, where black slaves were not considered citizens at all, but rather property owned by white masters.

Today, both countries have universal voting for adults over eighteen with no property or gender requirements. Sweden has greater voter participation at 80 percent, whereas in the United States, about 50 percent of eligible voters cast their ballot for president. According to U.S. Census, in 2000, only 38 percent of people under the poverty line voted. The elections of the president in the United States and prime minister in Sweden are really quite different processes. Sweden has a parliamentary system similar to that of Great Britain, Canada, and most European democracies. The election of a president in the United States is very different from the other democracies that came into being well after the United States was formed in 1790. There is no president in Sweden, but rather a prime minister who is part of the legislative body and elected by his or her political caucus, not by popular vote. There are no perpetual political campaigns like in the United States, with expensive television ads that attempt to "define" the opposing candidate, including his or her personal qualities, in the most negative way possible.

When the United States was formed in 1787 at the Constitutional Convention in Philadelphia, a major problem had to be confronted. The states already considered themselves autonomous entities that had fought against Great Britain under the Articles of Confederation, but found that those Articles proved inadequate as governing principles. Before "a more perfect union" could be accomplished, however, the smaller, poorer states had to be convinced that they would not be swallowed up or at least dominated by the larger, wealthier states like New York and Virginia. The larger, more prosperous states, in turn, did not want to be forced to share their wealth with the more numerous, smaller states if each state were to be given equal voting power. There was no contemporary model to follow.

To get all states on board, compromises had to be made. It was agreed that the new government would receive its enumerated powers from the people (not from the states) and that those powers not enumerated were reserved to the states. There would be two basically equal legislative bodies, House and Senate. To reflect the inherent power of the people, the House of Representatives would be elected every two years by the enfranchised voters of each state based on population. To protect the smaller states from being overwhelmed by the larger states, there would be two senators from each state, large or small, elected to six-year terms. The president, or chief executive, would be elected indirectly by state electors (the

Electoral College) for four-year terms by all the people of the individual states qualified to vote. The president, with the consent of the Senate, would appoint a Supreme Court with lifetime terms. It was not an ideal democracy of one-man, one-vote, but it permitted the survival of the fledgling nation.

Because some Americans have elevated the Constitution almost to holy writ, it should be emphasized that it was not a truly democratic document in the sense that all individuals were treated equally. Over half the people—women, Native Americans, slaves, and white men without property—were given no vote and, therefore, no protection or privileges. However, it unquestionably was a unique, progressive, groundbreaking document for its time, providing for amendments and subsequent court decisions that have allowed it to endure as the country's governmental framework for more than two hundred years. It may have fallen short of ideal, but as George Washington pragmatically declared at the time, it was about as good as could be expected and should be adopted, leaving to the future the making of corrections.

Sweden's evolution into a democracy with universal suffrage, guaranteed rights, and a written constitution took longer. It was spared America's trauma in fighting a war of independence to separate from another country and later an internal war that ripped the country apart and freed a large class of its people from chattel slavery.

Sweden also had a relatively long history of community democracy and national identity with a homogeneous stock of people and a national church that taught Christian values of love, brotherhood, and concern for the poor. Historically, most of its kings and nobles were elected. It was, however, a class society for centuries, which was formally reflected in its Rikstag. At the time the United States separated from Great Britain and created its written constitution,

Sweden, as mentioned earlier, had a strong king who shared power with nobles (we might call them warlords today) and a weak parliament, the Rikstag. In earlier centuries, there was a constant power struggle between the king, the nobles, and the Roman Catholic Church. After the Reformation, the Swedish Lutheran Church became the state church, and it had little secular power. Much later in the nineteenth century, the king and the nobles started to lose their power to labor unions, political parties, professional groups, farmers, and business interests. In 1865, at the time of America's Civil War, the Rikstag of four estates was replaced by a bicameral parliamentary body "of equal competence and authority," elected by common vote, which would meet annually but differed in property qualifications determining who was allowed to vote.

This was a historic reform, but nevertheless only 10 percent of the people had the right to vote because of gender and wealth requirements. There still were no political parties and universal voting, but that all changed in the twentieth century when women were given the vote in 1919 and when the Rikstag was changed from two chambers to a one-chamber legislative body in 1971. There was no formal written constitution until 1974. The basic Swedish belief about self-government, however, was the same as that held in the United States: all public power comes from the people, who select their representatives in free elections. Being smaller, Sweden doesn't have the complication of different states, each with its own constitution and laws.

The current government system in Sweden is called a constitutional monarchy, which really is a misnomer, particularly the monarchy part. The king is the symbolic and ceremonial head of state. His eldest child will inherit the throne, but he has no power to make any policy decisions or governmental appointments. What is recognized by all as "the government" is the prime minister and the ministers he or she appoints. The government is staffed by the prime minister's office, the various ministries and the Office for Administrative Affairs. Approximately 4,300 people work in government offices, some 160 of them political appointees.

Neither the American president nor the Swedish prime minister is elected by direct popular vote. The president is elected through the Electoral College, which can reflect less than the popular vote, as was the case for George W. Bush in 2000. The Swedish prime minister is elected by the members of his or her own party.

The prime minister forms "the government" by appointing his or her cabinet of ministers, who are usually, but not necessarily, members of the Rikstag. While they are serving in the government, however, their parliamentary seats are filled by substitutes chosen from their party.

The supreme authority, therefore, is the Rikstag, whose members are elected on an equal one-person, one-vote basis from electoral lists compiled by individual political parties. Any party is eligible to participate if it received at least 4 percent of the votes cast in the last election. The coalition of parties with the most votes selects the prime minister, who, in turn, selects the ministers, thus forming the cabinet that becomes the government that runs the country for the next four years. In the United States we call it the administration or the executive branch, and the top officials are appointed by the president with the concurrence of the Senate.

Two big differences between Sweden and the United States in their national elections are the unequal weight given to citizens' votes depending on their state's population and the treatment given smaller parties. In Sweden, all votes for the Rikstag are given equal weight. In the United States, votes for the House of Representatives, based on population, are also equal. However, votes for the Senate, based on the fact that there are two senators per state, regardless of population, are grossly unequal, and votes for the president based on the Electoral College are also unequal but less so. For example, the vote of a Nevada resident in a Senate election is worth about seventeen times that of a California resident. The vote of a Wyoming resident in the election for president is worth almost fourteen times the vote of a California resident.

Minority third parties in the United States really don't have a chance in presidential campaigns because it's winner-take-all in each state. The winner by either majority or plurality gets all the electoral votes in that state. A good example is the 1992 election involving Democrat Bill Clinton, Republican president George H. W. Bush, and Independent candidate Ross Perot. Although Perot polled 19 percent of the popular vote nationally (and higher than that in some states), he received no electoral votes because he was not the winner in any one state. Sweden's parliamentary elections are proportional. All parties winning more than 4 percent of the votes cast receive representation in the Rikstag. At present, seven parties are represented, ranging from the Green Party with 4.6 percent and the Social Democratic Party with 40 percent. All shades of political thought and interests are therefore represented. This is hardly true in the United States.

Another big difference between the two countries is the number of women in top elective office. In Sweden, 45 percent of the members of the Rikstag are women. In the United States Congress (House and Senate combined), 14 percent of seats are held by women. In my opinion as a former legislator, a greater number of women officeholders translates into better legislative priorities.

The national elections held every four years in Sweden don't come close to consuming proportionally the huge amounts of time and money spent in America. Candidates run as representatives of their political parties, so the party programs are the paramount issue, not the personality and appeal of the potential prime minister. Election lists are compiled by the party, so a candidate placed high enough on the party's list is automatically elected to the Rikstag, resulting in little need to raise large amounts of campaign money. Until recently the voters could choose only between parties, not individual candidates, although everyone knew that the chairman of the winning party would become prime minister. In 1998, a system was introduced that enabled voters to choose a particular candidate in addition to just choosing a party, but less than 30 percent of the voters did this and remained content to vote only for the party list. In order to bypass candidates higher up on a party's list, a candidate has to receive at least 8 percent of his or her party's ballots in an electoral district. Few have attempted this.

On the eve of the election there is a televised national debate between the leaders of the political parties, with the prime minister speaking first and the other parties each allotted time to challenge the government's record and explain their own program. The prime minister is then given a short time to reply to criticisms that have been raised.

On big controversial public issues, Sweden's constitution provides for nonbinding referendums that the government usually accepts as binding. In 1994, after a 52 percent yes vote, Sweden joined the European Union, and in 2003, after a 55 percent no vote, it declined to adopt the European currency, the euro. For years Swedes drove on the left side of the road, and a change to the right side was turned down by a referendum. But after the passage of a number of years the change to driving on the right was made by the government and was accepted without a big public fuss.

Major legislation and the reform in existing laws historically have been enacted nearly unanimously in Sweden because there has been a substantial period of public discussion and study by all parties, public and private.

Most legislative proposals are initiated by the government, but some come from individual Rikstag members, private citizens, special interest groups, or public authorities. Before a legislative proposal is formally drawn up for enactment, a commission of inquiry analyzes and evaluates it. The inquiry bodies, which operate independently of the government, may include private experts, public officials, and politicians; their report and conclusions are published and referred to all interested and affected bodies for comment. Only after this process is completed is a draft of a legislative bill prepared. The final responsibility for approving all new or amended legislation lies with the Rikstag, which refers all bills to one of the parliamentary committees for review and possible amendment. When the parliamentary committee has completed its deliberations, it submits a report, and, if approved, the bill is sent to the Rikstag for a final vote. If adopted, the bill becomes law. This process, of course, is different from that followed in the United States, where a legislative bill sometimes has little or no public scrutiny but nevertheless must pass both House and Senate in identical form and then must be signed by the president before it becomes law.

The role of our Supreme Court is different from Sweden's because of our court's unique power to nullify laws it has found unconstitutional by a majority vote of the nine nonelected justices. In Sweden this doesn't happen because appellate courts there can correct legislation and return it to the Rikstag for clarification, but the courts do not have authority to nullify laws. That remains a legislative prerogative.

An example of what mischief the United States Supreme Court can do to democratic elections is the famous case of *Buckley v. Valeo* (1976), in which the Court struck down most of the Federal Election Campaign Act of 1971 that put limits on the amounts an individual could spend on his or her own political campaign. By equating campaign spending with free speech, the Court ignored the corrupting effects unlimited campaign advertising has on a democracy, which, to function fairly, needs some semblance of political equality. It means that the superrich can finance their own campaigns even without showing any popular support. Campaign contributions are limited to avoid corruption, but campaign expenditures (advertising) are not restricted. Wealthy candidates consequently have more free speech than poor candidates.

Both Sweden and the United States are blessed to have representative democracies that encourage the free expression of ideas and political discussion. Sweden's government today is more transparent and has more inclination to foster consensus in governing, while in the United States there is more competition, more secrecy, and a winner-take-all attitude. Political combat has become much more divisive in the United States because there are only two viable national parties that seem to be sharply and evenly divided. To win political campaigns, so-called wedge issues that are personal and sometimes religiously based are raised to avoid public policy issues such as health care, taxation, poverty, education, the national debt, and Social Security.

While in Sweden in 2003, I asked a Swedish history professor if the issues of gun control and abortion had any impact or were discussed in Swedish national elections. He said, "No. I've heard about these interest groups active in America, but they are non-issues here."

A significant difference between political campaigns in Sweden and the United States is the role of money. In America, congressional representatives stand for election every two years and senators every six years. Once an incumbent is elected, fund-raising for the next election takes much of his or her time and energy, especially in competitive districts. Not all political contributors are interested in good government. Some have much narrower, but legitimate, reasons for contributing. As the cost of political campaigns rises, the need for money escalates and the role of the political lobbyist who provides access to government officials becomes more important. Corruption of the democratic system enters when money equates with political access. The recent criminal conviction of Republican lobbyist Jack Abramoff illustrates the point. In the United States, politics is drenched in money.

In Sweden, the pressure for raising substantial funds by candidates is less than in the United States because of Sweden's parliamentary system, which elevates political parties and their platforms over individual candidates. More important, the cost of campaigns is sharply reduced because political advertising on television and radio is prohibited. No free broadcasting time is given on either public or commercial stations, except for journalist-led questioning in special programs with party leaders during the final weeks before elections. In addition, there is, as noted earlier, a final television debate between party leaders two days before the election.

Sweden and the United States remain very similar in many ways, but in politics and political campaigns they are really quite different.

CHAPTER 12

Health Care

I N SWEDEN, everyone is guaranteed high-quality health care. Some is free of any charge and some requires token payment by consumers, but any charges are subsidized and limited so that easy, inexpensive access to care is universal. Public financing of health care is considered a social responsibility.

If you need emergency care, free treatment is available in the emergency room of any hospital. For regular medical care, make an appointment at the local health center and you should be able to see your family doctor within a week to ten days. If you feel ill and the situation is not too severe, the health center will give you help the same day without an appointment.

Health centers are organized to work as a team with physicians, nurses, auxiliary nurses, midwives, and physiotherapists. Your family doctor may refer you to a specialist if necessary, or you can go directly to a specialist without a referral. The cost of a consultation with your family physician is about $15.00. Fees for consulting a general practitioner in private practice could be more than twice as much. If you are admitted to a hospital, the fee charged is about $10.50 a day. To limit a patient's personal expense, there is a high-cost ceiling at which anyone who has paid a total of about $90.00 in health care charges is entitled to free medical care for the next twelve-month period.

Sweden shows great concern for the health and well-being of mothers and new babies by making all maternity care free. There are clinics for both child and maternal health. Staffed by midwives and physicians, maternity clinics provide regular checkups for expectant mothers during the entire pregnancy at no cost. The child clinics give vaccinations, health checks, consultations, and certain treatments free of charge to all children under school age. All medical and dental treatment for children and young people under twenty years of age is also free.

Adults must pay for their dental care, but costs are contained. Approximately half of Sweden's dentists agree to work within the national dental services, operated by local county councils, where the fees for basic procedures are fixed. The other dentists choose private practice and set their own fees. Whatever the charges for dental work, the state pays 40 percent of basic care, including crowns and bridges. For more extensive procedures for those over sixty-five, there are special protections that limit the cost for the individual.

There are 900 state-run "Apotekets" or pharmacies nationwide, which are the only places you can fill a prescription from a doctor or midwife. Prescriptions are subsidized by the state to keep them from being prohibitively expensive. If you have a condition that requires extensive prescription drug treatment, you can get a card to record your purchases, and if you spend over approximately $180 in a calendar year, further purchases for that year are free.

By any standard, health among Swedes is very good. Infant mortality is low at three deaths per thousand in the first year of life. In the United States, it's eight deaths per thousand. Life expectancy in Sweden is eighty years, and in the U.S. life expectancy is seventy-seven.

What is attractive about the Swedish health system is that it is high quality and low cost for both the country and the consumer; most important, it is universal.

One reason health care is inexpensive in Sweden is the narrow gap in salaries between health care professionals. The average monthly salary for a nurse is about $2,200, while a hospital physician with a specialty has a salary of about $4,600.

To compare the Swedish health care system with that of the United States is almost impossible. That is because Sweden *has* a system and the United States does not—or more accurately, it has many, many systems, depending on one's age, wealth, insurance or lack thereof, and locality. To call the delivery of health care in the United States a system is an oxymoron. It does, however, deliver health care and most of it is high quality and nearly universal. It's not really a system, but more a hodgepodge.

For one thing, it's very expensive. America spends almost double what Sweden does on health care. In 2004, a United Nations study reported that the United States spent $4,887 per capita for health care while Sweden spent $2,270 per capita. Its system is uniform and efficient and consequently less expensive than in the United States, where health care is inefficient and very, very expensive. That is because the U.S. "system" is a patchwork involving thousands of different providers and hundreds of different insurance companies and HMOs, each striving to make a profit for its shareholders, often while paying huge executive salaries. This "free-market"-driven portion of the U.S. "system" costs too much and leaves a lot of people unprotected. Those who are excluded because they have no insurance and/or are too poor to pay do two things: they delay seeking medical treatment until the situation becomes catastrophic, or they get help through publicly funded sources such as Medicaid (insurance for the poor) or hospital emergency rooms or through a haphazard "safety net" of state and local clinics and centers that are funded by local taxes. This is very inefficient, particularly with regard to services obtained through hospital emergency rooms. Some Americans pride themselves in not having "socialized medicine," but today public or socialized expenditures for health care almost equal what Americans spend for private health care. (Think Medicare, Medicaid, and the Veterans Administration.) In fact, America seems to provide health care for everyone in one fashion or another. The poor are not abandoned to die in the streets. Through municipal or charitable hospitals or facilities, there is a ragged localized "safety net" that will help those unable to pay. These facilities are usually dependent on public funds, so the cost is eventually borne by the taxpayers. In sum, the so-called health care system in the United States is nearly universal but is also very inefficient and therefore very expensive.

Those at greatest risk in this crazy-quilt system are typically the middle class under age sixty-five who have lost health insurance they once had through their employment. They are not old enough to qualify for Medicare and not poor enough to quality for Medicaid. The wealthy, the elderly, and the poor receive the care they need, but those in between have to pay expensive insurance premiums and copayments out of their own pocket or risk disaster.

The majority of the uninsured are neither poor by official standards nor unemployed. They are contract workers whose employers offer no fringe benefits, single working mothers, and others who find it impossible to pay the high monthly premiums out of their paychecks.

R. King Hillier, director of legislative relations for Harris County in Houston, Texas, was quoted recently in the *New York Times* as saying, "Now it's hitting people who look like you and me, dress like you and me, drive nice cars and live in nice houses but can't afford $1,000 a month for health insurance for their families." Another Texas man, a forty-one-year-old accountant, is employed but lost his health insurance when his company went bust three years ago. He saw a doctor about difficulty in swallowing, but has not taken some additional tests ordered by his doctor. He said, "I was supposed to go back after the x-ray results came, but decided just to live with it for awhile. I may just be a walking time bomb."

The number of uninsured Americans continues to rise. In the year 2002, according to the U.S. Census Bureau, 15.2 percent of the population (43.6 million people) are uninsured. Even many full-time workers—an astonishing 20 million—lack health coverage.

The so-called health care system in the United States is truly unique and truly expensive. According to the Human Development Reports of the United Nations for 2004, the United States spent 14 percent of its gross domestic product on health expenditures. Sweden spent 8.8 percent. The other industrialized countries, such as Great Britain, Germany, France, Canada, and the other Scandinavian countries, all have a single-payer system similar to Sweden's. These countries help their industries to be more competitive by not burdening employers with the high cost of providing health insurance for their workers. General Motors claims that this costs them an additional $15,000 per year per worker and continues to move their production to Canada. The United States stands alone in not recognizing that universal health care is a national responsibility requiring a uniform nonprofit national solution.

CHAPTER 13

Wealth Distribution

ABOUT TWENTY-FIVE YEARS AGO I was with a Swedish cousin who was visiting the United States for the first time. We were driving around Minneapolis/St. Paul near the University of Minnesota and the Mississippi River. A nice part of town. My Swedish was almost nonexistent and his English was not much better, so at first I had difficulty understanding his question. Maybe that is why I remember it so vividly. The question was, "Do you have homeless people in the United States?"

The question was understandable. He had heard about this phenomenon but was skeptical that it could exist in a country as prosperous as ours. I told him there might be a few homeless in other parts of the country, but I didn't know of any in the Twin Cities. In fact, I had seen a few people in New York City and San Francisco shuffling along the sidewalk, pushing grocery carts or carrying bags, but I assumed they were mentally ill or on drugs. To me, at that time, the homeless were invisible.

All that has changed. Nationwide we know the homeless are no longer just those who are suffering from mental disability or substance abuse. There are thousands throughout the country, and the number is growing. For most homeless people, the answer is simply that they have no money. They have no family support, no savings, no trust fund, no pension, and there is no adequate safety net for them. Many are the working poor, and many have children. Figures are hard to come by, but the *Economist* reported that between 700,000 and 800,000 people are homeless in America on any given night.

Much is being done by individual cities, counties, states, charities, and congregations to provide temporary shelter, but the tide continues to rise.

The work ethic has not died in America. In fact, as a nation we work more hours per week than Western Europeans. We are the richest nation on earth, with the largest gross domestic product. The problem for all of society is how this income is distributed. In their excellent recent book, *Wealth and Our Commonwealth,* (2002) William H. Gates Sr. (Bill Gates's dad) and Chuck Collins pull no punches in describing this maldistribution:

> The United States is now the most unequal society in the industrialized world. The richest fifth of Americans earn eleven times more than the bottom fifth. At the bottom end of the of the pay scale, the number of people working for poverty wages is troubling. The estimated "living wage" meant to lift a wage earner out of poverty, is now at least ten dollars an hour; the federal minimum wage is stalled at just over half that amount. . . .
>
> At the same time, the incomes of the top one-fifth of households increased steeply and the income of the top one percent has skyrocketed. (p. 14)

The gap between high-paid executives and the average wage earner has continued to spread dramatically.

According to *Business Week* magazine, the disparity between the highest-paid executives in the 365 largest companies and their employees in 1980 was forty-two to one. Today the ratio is over four hundred to one.

This is hard to believe, I know, but what is harder to believe is that these huge pay packages were given to many executives whose corporations' performances were mediocre or worse. (Think Enron, WorldCom, Tyco, Global Crossing, Adelphia.) The fallout has been the anger and disillusionment of workers and stockholders immediately affected. This version of "buddy capitalism," whereby top executives appoint the members of the corporate board that sets these incredible compensation packages and then doles out generous perks to themselves, should shake the faith of everyone. Such a disparity in income between workers and top management doesn't exist in Sweden for a number of reasons. First, the unions, which are very strong, and the employers' organizations, which are also very strong, would not allow it. In addition, it is not part of the ingrained culture of Swedes to tolerate, much less encourage, this kind of excess. As discussed in Chapter 1, an important principle is expressed by the Swedish word *lagom*, which has its roots in the Viking days, when people drank from a common bowl. It was understood that each person drank lagom—not too much, but just enough, so as to leave enough for others. The importance of sharing and moderation is honored and respected today in all aspects of Swedish society. Showy or excessive spending is not a trait the Swedes admire. There is no enforced uniformity, and of course there are some who achieve greater wealth than others, but gross excess in anything is to be avoided.

An even more disturbing contrast between Sweden and the United States is the inequality in savings and wealth. Savings is what people have to fall back on in economic downturns and personal disasters. Savings also allow people to get ahead—pay for education, buy a home, or start a small business. In the United States, the savings rate is dangerously low. Given current economic trends, that's understandable, however.

Again, from Gates and Collins in *Wealth and Our Commonwealth*, speaking about the United States today:

In terms of financial wealth, including the ownership of stocks, bonds, and other investments, the top 1 percent of households own 47 percent and the top 20 percent own 91 percent. The benefits of the economic boom of the last two decades were highly skewed to the top. Between 1983 and 1998, almost all the growth in wealth of the economic boom went to the top 20 percent of households. Over the same time period, the wealth of the bottom 40 percent of households showed an absolute decline. (pp. 15–16)

In the three decades after World War II, both the United States and Sweden pursued public policies that shared prosperity and equality of opportunity. The GI Bill that educated millions of returning veterans in college at public expense and federal home mortgage insurance proved to be extremely popular and effective national investments. The interstate highway system created in the 1950s during the Eisenhower administration was another public investment that created enormous national wealth. Sweden and the United States were moving in parallel in prosperity and providing equality for their citizens.

What has happened since is one of the dramatic contrasts between the two countries today. In terms of division of wealth, Sweden is one of the countries with the most equality. While it pains me to say it, I must report that the United States has the most unequal society in the industrial world with more money per capita and at the same time more poverty per capita. The 2003 *Human Development Report* of the United Nations Development Programme, published by Oxford University, ranked seventeen high-income industrialized countries belonging to the Organisation for Economic Co-operation and Development according to a human poverty index. Sweden ranked number one with the least poverty and the United States ranked seventeenth with the most poverty. Norway, Finland, the Netherlands, and Denmark were right behind Sweden.

In the early 1990s, well after the establishment of its welfare state, Sweden's economy hit a rough patch along with other countries. Unemployment shot up to 10 percent, its highest in decades. Critics predicted the unraveling of its social service system. But after intense discussion and several political elections that resulted in some adjustment to the system, recovery returned. There was no upheaval. Consensus democracy responded. In the late 1990s, Sweden shared the economic upturn with other industrial nations, and the unemployment rate dropped to around 5 percent, where it remained for recent years. Both Sweden and the United States in 2006 have around 5 percent unemployment. This is better than in Europe overall, which has over 8 percent. The welfare state in Sweden is robust and flexible and continues on its path of social equality while the difference between Sweden and the United States continues to grow.

Most of this drift toward inequality in the United States grew from the right-wing idea that taxation for social purposes like public education, universal health care, and a safety net for the needy and elderly was a wasteful subsidy that undercut the self-reliance and independence the early settlers possessed and upon which the nation was built. Taxation for military expenditures was, at the same time, seen as justified in preventing the spread of worldwide communism. The same thinking has been dominant today during the current Bush administration, although the word terrorism has been substituted for the word communism.

According to the Economic Policy Institute, the ratio of income received by a nation's top 10 percent to those in the lowest 10 percent is greater in the United States than in any other industrial nation. The ratio in the United States is 5.6; in Canada it is 3.9, and Sweden's ratio is 2.6.

At the present time, the major contrast between Sweden and the United States is actually a matter of emphasis. Both have "free market" capitalistic economies. The Swedes look upon the government as the neutral guarantor of social fairness and equality of opportunity that requires a system in place to maintain it. Taxation, which ensures that everyone gets a chance to develop his or her talent and enjoy basic living standards for life, is accepted and not considered an evil intrusion upon individual liberty imposed by an oppressive government. Taxation is okay to fund the military for the defense of its borders and some international peacekeeping missions sponsored by the United Nations, but nothing more.

In the United States today, right-wing conservatives believe that tax cuts for the rich that allow greater "capital formation," together with the "invisible hand" of the market, free from any government interference, will work their magic and deliver greater equality and social benefits for all. Under this vision, poor people will achieve more on their own and be stronger because of it.

Quite a different vision of democracy, isn't it? For the past twenty-five years the Swedish model appears to be doing a better job for all of its citizens.

Since 2000, under the current Republican administration, tax policies have made the superrich even richer with income tax cuts in 2001 and 2002 and repeal of the estate tax that exclusively benefits the heirs of multimillionaires (it's now being called "the Paris Hilton tax"). If you point out this truth it raises cries of fomenting class warfare and attempting to punish the successful. Nevertheless, many successful, intelligent, patriotic, wealthy people see the absurdity and the danger of creating an aristocracy of inheritors in these policies and have spoken out against them. They include people like

Warren Buffett, Bill Gates Sr., Paul Newman, George Soros, and Ted Turner.

Before he became a Supreme Court justice, Louis Brandeis said that "we can have a democratic society or we can have great concentrated wealth in the hands of a few. We cannot have both."

Brandeis was right.

CHAPTER 14

Old Age Security

BEFORE THERE WAS A WELFARE STATE in Sweden and the New Deal in the United States (in the 1930s), old age meant poverty for many in both countries, except for the wealthy, privileged classes. The few exceptions were those with military pensions and those whose larger, paternalistic employers provided substantial pensions. Most old folks, Swedish and American, had to rely on family to care for them. This was one rationalization for large families, but that trend has become a thing of the past in both the United States and Sweden. Today, most older individuals in both countries live apart from their families, which is quite different from many other parts of the world.

The Great Depression of the 1930s provided the shock needed to move both nations to undertake a universal old age security system that would prevent poverty for retired and elderly citizens. Unlike the U.S., Sweden had had a modest old age pension for the poor for many years, based on a model borrowed from the Germans, but it was not universal.

In 1935, Franklin Roosevelt signed into law the Social Security Act, which, among other provisions, established old age benefits for retired workers in commerce and industry, but not originally for farmers or the self-employed. You have to make contributions for ten years to draw pension benefits. It never was intended to be a full retirement pension system but rather more of a "safety net."

In 1946, Sweden's retirement pension was substantially revised.

Along with the construction of its welfare state, the pensions became truly universal by removing any means test, and the program was funded through pay-as-you-go contributions by employers and employees. It received unanimous support in Parliament at the time and has undergone several stages of development since. Its relatively modest benefits invited increased political pressure from working people for increases closer to the level of a pensioner's income before retirement. The dominant Social Democratic Party was receptive to these proposals. The 1960s and '70s brought increased prosperity to the country, which was when Sweden established a more generous welfare state that eliminated poverty and stressed equality.

In 1957, after considerable public debate, the government held a nonbinding referendum offering three pension alternatives, each with a different mix of governmental or public administration. None of these alternatives won a majority, but the Social Democratic Party's alternative won a plurality and after the Parliamentary election it formed a government that adopted their two-pension system, which became law in 1960.

This two-tier system combined an increased basic pension with a new defined benefit plan based on a worker's earnings over time. Both components were linked to a cost-of-living index. Because there was general prosperity in Sweden at the time, this reform had the desired effect of increasing the income of the retired elderly population and effectively reducing poverty and inequality in the country.

Unfortunately, the cost-of-living indexing of the benefits and increased longevity of the population made its solvency unstable, and the need for further reform became obvious. This also is where the United States is today: long-term solvency is in danger.

In characteristic Swedish fashion, a parliamentary commission was appointed in 1984 to study and define the problem. This process eventually resulted in a comprehensive report on the status in 1994 outlining the need for reform of the pension system. The report served as a basis for public and parliamentary debate. A fundamentally new pension system was adopted in 1998 and was scheduled to be fully phased in by 2003. The legislation cut across divisions in left and right political blocs and was eventually supported by over 80 percent in Parliament.

This new pension, which is in effect today, is incredibly complex and detailed but has been hailed as a success in guaranteeing a basic safety net for all retirees, giving some private investment choices to others, and maintaining solvency for the foreseeable future.

Contributions of 18.5 percent of payroll earnings are divided into two accounts, with 16 percent going into an account that forms the worker's pension based on work history, and 2.5 percent being deposited into an individual investment account. The benefit formula in the larger account is linked to a worker's contribution and his or her life expectancy at retirement (although the pension is lifelong for each individual). The smaller, basic "safety net" pension is guaranteed to all, regardless of contributions.

To ensure solvency, payment of both the "safety net" pension and the larger pension based on employment history and contributions is linked to national economic growth to ensure solvency.

The 2.5 percent dedicated to private investment accounts allows each person to select his or her fund manager from among five options, thus introducing for the first time an element of individual choice and individual risk. To date, most Swedes let the 2.5 percent money go into a default account maintained by the government because the investment choices seem too complex and overwhelming. These new private investment accounts in Sweden are savings on top of the regular pensions and paid by an additional 2.5 percent of wages split between worker and employer. There is no diversion of funds that undermines the existing system, as has been proposed by President Bush.

The differences between Sweden's government-run pensions and the United States' old age benefits under Social Security are striking in three ways:

- Sweden's anticipated solvency;
- the universality of its plan; and
- the sufficiency of the Swedish plan for those of little or no means.

Projected solvency represents the biggest difference between the two countries' systems. As the United States' deficit grows and the older population increases, an ominous cloud expands that threatens all future retirees and the country itself. We are not alone. Most Western European countries have a similar problem.

According to the U.S. Census, the "older old" are increasing disproportionately in each age bracket over sixty-five because there used to be relatively fewer people in those brackets. By the year 2040, for example, it's projected that the number of those between ages sixty-five and seventy-four will increase somewhat, but those over eighty-five will grow a whopping 240 percent. By the same year Americans aged eighty and over will outnumber children under age five.

In the United States today, few people can be expected to live on Social Security benefits alone after age sixty-five. In 2003, the monthly Social Security check for the average retired worker was $900. If a person's lifetime average annual payroll earnings in 2003 was $60,000, the approximate benefit would be $1,751 a month or $21,013 annually, about one-third the wages prior to retirement. A person without an additional private pension, substantial savings, or a trust fund is in big trouble!

Peter G. Peterson, a banker and economist, and Richard Nixon's secretary of commerce, has sounded the alarm in his trenchant books, *Gray Dawn: How the Coming Age Wave Will Transform America—And the World* (1999) and *Running on Empty: How the Democratic and Republican Parties Are Bankrupting Our Future and What Americans Can Do about It* (2004). All developed nations, including the United States, are on a collision course toward this unseen iceberg of global aging. With prosperity and better health care, the older population in developed countries is growing and the younger working population is shrinking. This means that the benefits paid to today's retirees cannot be sustained for future retirees without making drastic changes—and soon. *Fortunately for the Swedish population, this problem has been acknowledged, studied, discussed, and seriously met.* In the United States, most political leaders have been in denial. Our national deficits in the budget and foreign trade continue to grow while, unbelievably, the necessary taxes to solve domestic problems have been continually cut by the present Bush administration.

If the United States decides to address the problem of strengthening Social Security retirement pensions, increased funding is essential. Diverting money out of present funding to establish new private accounts would only make matters worse. The amount deducted from workers and their employers to fund "social security" (presently 12.4 percent of wages) is woefully inadequate because only about 7.2 percent of this money is set aside for retirement pensions. The balance of 5.3 percent is used by the Social Security Administration for disability and survivor benefits. *To compare funding for purely retirement benefits between the two countries, the figures are 16 percent of wages in Sweden and 7.2 percent of wages in the United States. No wonder Sweden has a fiscally sound retirement system and the United States does not.* In fairness, it must be said that Sweden's pension system awards greater benefits and is more universal, but it is clear that the less generous U.S. system is substantially underfunded.

What works in Sweden may not work in America. But what is crucial is that increased aging be recognized and met as a national problem. Funding Medicare is even more serious than Social Security's pension problem, and continued deficits just dig a deeper hole. What was once just an issue for "poor folks" has rapidly become one for all of us in the United States unless we're extremely wealthy.

CHAPTER 15

Economic Health:
A Mixed Prognosis

SWEDEN IS A HIGHLY INDUSTRIALIZED COUNTRY with a small domestic market, making it extremely dependent on exports, which account for roughly 45 percent of its gross domestic product. In today's globalized world Sweden has prospered and had its economic ups and downs along with Western Europe and the United States. Most of its increase was driven by innovations and investment. During the second half of the twentieth century, for example, two successful auto manufacturers, Saab and Volvo, and a large producer of household appliances, Electrolux, developed. What was remarkable was Sweden's ability to maintain a narrow differential between upper and lower wages while building a universal safety net and funding new and expanded social programs. This could only be accomplished through cooperation between the government led by the Social Democrats working with strong labor unions and strong employers' organizations.

In the public sphere, money was spent on highways and public transportation, such as modern trains and the excellent Stockholm subway system, started in the 1950s. This postwar dynamic period of growth and prosperity lasted until the end of the 1960s. To put the growth of Sweden's economy in a larger historical perspective, between 1870 and 1970 it had the fastest growth in the world after Japan.

In the early 1970s, Sweden, in parallel with world trends, went through economic changes when high wages, high taxes, and inflation drove manufacturing costs up and consequently exports down. The OPEC embargo in 1973 made things worse because of higher oil prices. The country was in recession, and in reaction, non-socialist conservatives won the elections in 1976. But since they did no better, the more liberal Social Democrats returned to power in 1982. By the late 1980s, new trouble came when there was another upswing caused temporarily by a bubble funded on credit. The economy "overheated," and the conservative parties returned with a program of tax cuts and some limited changes in welfare benefits. The national debt grew alarmingly, and the Social Democrats returned again in 1994. With some combination of skill and luck they rode the general global upswing of the 1990s (the so-called Clinton years) and remain in power pending the 2006 national election.

The beginning of the twenty-first century has brought strength and promise to the Swedish economy. It has retained its vitality and egalitarianism in the increasingly globalized world. Its highly educated open society, in which most people are fluent in English (the international language of business and science) has prepared it for the new century. The country's GDP continues to grow, and unemployment is relatively low. The national debt is low and declining. All these benchmarks are better than for most other European countries. The confidence Swedes have in the future of their economy was demonstrated in 2002 when they declined by referendum to adopt the euro as their currency, even though they remain members of the European Union.

All studies and surveys indicate a positive economic future for Sweden and the Nordic region. The UN's International Telecommunication Union reported in December 2003 that Sweden and the other Nordic nations lead the world in digital technology access. The IDC/World Times Information Society Index for the fourth year in a row ranked Sweden as the number one country with the strongest position to take full advantage of the Information Revolution because of its advanced information, computer, Internet, and social infrastructures. In 2003, the World Economic Forum, a Geneva-based economic think tank, ranked Sweden's economy the third most competitive in the world, behind Finland and the United States. According to the Organisation for Economic Co-operation and Development, Sweden invests more in knowledge enhancement, including spending on education programs and research and development, than any other country. The United States ranks seventeenth in this regard.

Richard Florida, formerly a professor at Carnegie Mellon University, now at George Mason University, studies the growth of cities and countries that attract "creative" people who will likely contribute to continuing prosperity. In ranking countries by a "creative index," Florida considers factors such as a nation's investment in research and development, number of patents issued, and the proportion of people with university educations, as well as a country's social tolerance and ethnic diversity. His most current rankings put Sweden first, just ahead of the United States, with Finland, the Netherlands, and Denmark rounding out his top five.

Compared to the United States' wealth or gross domestic product, Sweden's national wealth per capita was $33,890 in 2005. The GDP per person in the United States in 2005 was $37,240, or significantly greater. But wait a minute—who owns this wealth? As shown in earlier chapters, this national wealth is spread very differently in Sweden than in America. Among seventeen industrial countries ranked by the 2004 United Nations *Human Development Report,* the United States has the greatest per capita poverty and Sweden has the least. When other elements of the economy and public spending are considered in addition to the amount of poverty, Sweden ranks second, just behind Norway in the overall Human Development Index, and the United States ranks eighth. This report graphically affirms the conclusion that the United States has great wealth that works very well for those at the top but very poorly for many on the bottom. At the same time, Sweden's smaller per capita national wealth seems to work for everyone.

Moving away from the question of wealth distribution to the continuing economic health of America, there are some glaring weaknesses that should be honestly recognized and addressed if America's overall economic health is to be maintained. Without denigrating the United States' economic achievements to date, here are, in my opinion, some of those weaknesses:

- Ballooning national debt;
- Crony capitalism;
- Health care drain; and
- Increased defense spending.

Ballooning National Debt

The combination of an economic slowdown, tax cuts, and higher government spending has turned America's budget around. During 2000, the last year of the Clinton administration, the federal government had a *surplus* of 2.4 percent of GDP. By fiscal 2003, the budget had been reversed and reached a *deficit* of 3.5 percent of GDP. The *Economist's* poll of industrial countries reported the amount of debt (current account) for the United States in 2004 to be 5.1 percent of GDP.

The International Monetary Fund warned in January 2004 that rising budget deficits and trade deficits caused a shaky fiscal foundation that should be repaired. The IMF argued that the United States would have to raise taxes or reduce spending, or both, to bring its finances under control and that recovery from the recession alone would not do it.

Robert E. Rubin, former secretary of the treasury, said in a paper issued independent of the IMF report that the federal budget was "on an unsustainable path" and that the "scale of the nation's projected budgetary imbalance is now so large that the risk of severe adverse consequences must be taken very seriously."

Here are two remarkable figures. In the 2000 fiscal year, when President George W. Bush came to power, the country had a budget surplus of $236 billion. In 2004, the budget deficit was $520 billion: an incredible turnaround of $756 billion. The nonpartisan Concord Coalition assessed the fiscal responsibility of Congress and the Bush administration for 2003 and concluded, "In summary, long-term revenue declines (tax cuts), combined with no sign of spending restraint, mean massive deficits every year for at least the next decade."

The worldwide financial markets up to now have shown faith in the United States' political maturity and have given the country the benefit of the doubt. But sooner or later increased U.S. deficits and the unwillingness of its political leaders to rein them in will drive interest rates up, which, in turn, will threaten its productivity growth. Being the world's strongest military power can't protect us from this happening and may exacerbate it.

Crony Capitalism

In theory, a free market economy should work well for all of its constituencies, entrepreneurs (creators), investors (owners), managers, and workers. In very small businesses, these categories may be merged in one person or family. In large corporations, they usually are quite separate. To be successful there has to be some consensus or balance on how each constituent element should be "fairly" paid or rewarded. If no consensus can be reached on this issue or if some gross distortion occurs through disaster, incompetence, dishonesty, or a power imbalance, the entire enterprise will likely fail.

Examples of this are the many well publicized business failures of Enron, WorldCom, Adelphia, and Dynegy. But beyond these examples of fraud and illegality, there are many, many examples of greed that are legal but very harmful to our economy. The United States relies heavily on inflows of foreign capital that depends upon international faith in the integrity of U.S. companies and financial markets.

Twenty-five years ago, CEO compensation in large corporations was forty times the average worker's pay, but now it is often four hundred to five hundred times more. This sea change affects our entire free market system and economic health as a country.

In his business column in *Newsweek* (May 5, 2003), Robert J. Samuelson wrote: "CEOs justify their compensation by saying they get what the 'market dictates,' just like everyone else. Rubbish. Their market is highly artificial. Compensation levels are what economists call 'administered prices' set by corporate directors who are usually top executives or retired executives. The result is an artificial welfare system designed to ensure that even mediocre top executives do well." If executives are overcompensated in stock options, which is very common, they are tempted to raise stock prices by stretching accounting rules to puff up profits in the short term, but that tactic weakens the company in the long term, cheats stockholders, demoralizes workers, and scares investors.

Unfortunately, corporate boards in America routinely practice various forms of crony capitalism that is a drain on its economy.

Health Care Drain

Another drain on America's economy is the extraordinary amount of money that is spent on both public and private health care. This is because in the United States there is an expensive patchwork system of hundreds of private for-profit insurance companies, HMOs, hospitals, drug companies, and thousands of health care providers, each with its own administrative bureaucracy and advertising budgets. (See Chapter 12.)

The U.S. Department of Health and Human Services reported that spending for health care rose from 14.1 percent of GDP in 2001 to almost 15 percent (14.9) in 2002. The percentage of GDP spent on health care in Sweden in 2002 was 7.9 percent, half as much.

Public spending on health care such as Medicare, Medicaid, and the Veterans Administration already amounts to about 45 percent of all health care spending in the United States. In other industrial countries, public spending averages 72 percent. Constantly rising health care costs drain the U.S. economy, squeezing both employers and employees and causing increasingly bitter labor relations.

Increased Defense Spending

Whether the goal is characterized as world leadership or world domination, the United States has committed itself to huge financial obligations that, in public discourse, have been labeled "defense spending." Since September 11, 2001, and particularly since the invasion of Iraq in March 2003, the pressure for increased defense spending has become irresistible. Neither the Democratic nor the Republican Party wants to run the risk of being tagged as "weak on defense," a label both parties consider toxic. "Defense spending," of course, has been expanded to the "War on Terror," which in turn has been widened to include the war in Iraq and that country's reconstruction—even though that war did not lessen terror around the world, but actually increased those dangers.

But my point is that for the foreseeable future, "defense spending" will inevitably shoulder aside other priorities that are needed to maintain a healthy economy, such as increased public expenditure for education at all levels.

When you step back and compare the economies of the two countries, Sweden remains the healthier of the two because it spends less on inefficient health care, inefficient capitalism, increasing interest on national debt, and constantly growing military expenditures. There is obvious danger ahead for the United States.

CHAPTER 16

Family Support

THE FAMILY SUPPORT SYSTEM in Sweden recognizes the crucial importance of children to their nation's future. It includes health care, education, and financial support that is universal and not just given to families in need. The fact that it is universal blunts class distinctions, makes it easier to administer, and gives everyone a stake in its success. (This isn't a rigid system, but more of a national consensus.)

The Swedish system provides free medical care for all mothers and children before and after childbirth. There are maternity clinics for both children and mothers staffed by midwives and physicians who give regular checkups to expectant mothers during their entire pregnancy and childbirth at no cost. Child clinics give vaccinations, health checks, consultations, and treatments to all children under school age. This universal care apparently works well because infant mortality is very low at three deaths per thousand births in the first year of life.

Sweden encourages its people to have more babies, who they hope will grow up to be healthy, productive, tax-paying citizens. Each family is paid a monthly nontaxable allowance of $152 for each child until the age of sixteen or until the child graduates from high school. Additional payments are made to large families that have more than three children. (My wife and I should have moved to Sweden. We had eight children.)

In addition to being paid to have more babies, parents are

encouraged to take paid parental leave to stay home and care for the baby during the first year of life. This is particularly helpful for mothers because most Swedish women work and would find it difficult to lose needed income if they took extended child care leaves without pay. Under the parental leave law, the two parents are allowed combined leaves totaling sixteen months while receiving 80 percent of their previous salary for the first 390 days and for the remaining 90 days a flat rate of $8 per day. Parents who were not employed receive $19.50 per day for the first 390 days and the same $8 rate thereafter as everyone else. The cost of the parental leave benefit is paid by the state, *not* by the employer. Each parent must use at least sixty days, and the balance can be allocated over several years, however the couple decides. This is an attempt to encourage all Swedish fathers to stay home and provide child care for at least two months. There is also a similar reimbursement for income loss up to sixty days if you need to stay home to care for a sick child under twelve years of age.

The entire parental leave program is voluntary, but the incentive to participate is attractive and widely used. Usually the mother, apart from the two months allocated to the father, is the one who takes most of the leave. But this is not always the case. I met a young Australian father on a lake excursion boat in southern Sweden near the city of Växjö. He was on this outing with his toddler son, and in our conversation he explained that he had married a Swedish woman who earned more money on her job than he did, so he was taking the greater part of the parental leave. (He had been a well-paid police officer in Australia but had not yet qualified for a similar position in Sweden and was working part-time and taking Swedish language classes.)

Under the Swedish law, the two months of benefits the father rejects are forfeited and cannot be used by the mother. It is up to the parents to decide, so I can only imagine that some tense discussions between parents occasionally result.

Further public support for families is given in the form of preschool education. The aim is twofold: to encourage children's early development and to enable parents to combine parenthood with work or studies, a particularly important feature for women. Participation is voluntary and is not entirely free. Children are registered and parents pay a flexible fee or tuition based on income, but which is capped at $150 a month. Lower-income families pay less, and higher-income families are not required to pay more than the $150 ceiling. All preschool programs are nationwide and open to all. They are extensively subsidized and staffed with qualified, well-trained teachers. Almost all children (76 percent) are in some type of preschool education. The very early childhood programs are roughly similar to Head Start in the United States, a program targeted to selected children in poverty.

Family support does not end here. In my opinion, the entire educational system, from preschool through college, is part of the Swedish family support system. As noted earlier, there is a monthly child allowance paid to parents for all students in elementary and secondary education. After graduating from high school and going on to college or some other postsecondary training, students pay no tuition and can receive grants and low-interest loans for housing and other expenses that are made without reference to the economic situation of the student's parents or spouse. About 40 percent of young people in Sweden go on to higher education within five years after completing high school. In other words, a Swedish family doesn't need a ton of money or go deeply into debt to send a qualified child to college.

If the high school graduate decides not to go on to higher education, she or he is well equipped to enter the job market. During

172 → EARL GUSTAFSON

the final three years a variety of special classes can be taken that train a student for immediate employment. By that time the student is reasonably fluent in English, which is a required subject beginning in the third grade. If you are lost in Sweden, it is best to ask a young person or someone like a sales clerk or bank teller who deals with the public—they all speak English.

A big contrast between Sweden and the United States can be made by looking at the impact of education expenses on the average family. In the United States, to send a child to a good college, public or private, you should have substantial accumulated wealth or a child especially talented academically or athletically.

→ CHAPTER 17 ←

Taxation

A NY ATTEMPT TO COMPARE Sweden with the United States must touch on the issue of taxation. I'll try to avoid getting lost in numbing minutiae. As discussed in earlier chapters, Sweden has taken on large public responsibilities that lay claim to an equally large portion of the country's resources. According to the OEDC, Sweden's tax revenue in 2004 was the equivalent of 50 percent of GDP compared to 25 percent of GDP in the United States. Some of Sweden's taxes are returned in the form of direct payments for child allowances and for funding various services like free education, universal health care, and old age pensions. In the Euro area, tax revenues on average reach 40 percent of GDP.

The tax system in Sweden, with its income taxes, sales taxes, and property taxes, is not very different from taxes in the United States. One aspect that is very different and should be remembered when comparing the two countries' taxes is the fact that America has fifty states, each with its own taxes that vary from state to state and are collected in addition to federal taxes. Sweden, being much smaller, has basically one national system with only the income tax varying slightly in administration and rates among localities.

In the United States, for example, most states have an income tax, some do not; most have a sales tax, but rates even in individual cities may vary substantially.

In Sweden, taxes on individual income are graduated and start at about 20 percent but only after some basic deductions are allowed for low-income taxpayers and pensioners. All who earn more than $2,100 a year are required to pay some income tax. In addition, a special tax reduction or credit is granted to those with earned income under $17,550, and this credit is gradually reduced in size and eliminated completely when income reaches $32,000. The top marginal rate for taxable income over $50,750 is 49 percent, higher than the marginal rate in the United States, which is 28 percent over $143,500 of adjusted gross income. The United States allows much higher "itemized" deductions, such as interest paid on mortgages, and doesn't reach its very top rate of 35 percent until taxable income totals $312,000.

As in the United States, there are payroll deductions in Sweden for old age pensions. These deductions are 7 percent and are matched by the employer for a total 14 percent. In addition, 2.5 percent is deducted and set aside in a personal investment account, which allows each person to select his or her fund manager from among five choices but does not jeopardize the long-term funding of the regular pension system. Tax on corporate income is 28 percent, considerably lower than United States' rate of 39 percent.

All income earned from capital, such as dividend interest and rent received, is taxed at 30 percent. Only one-half of capital gains from the sale of property, such as stock or real estate, is taxed. It is possible to defer the tax on the sale of a residence if the seller purchases a similar property within one year.

According to a Fact Sheet published in 2004 by the Swedish Institute titled "Financial Circumstances of Swedish Households," the average monthly income of a full-time industrial worker in 2003 was $2,580, or $30,960 annually. The average monthly wage of a white-collar employee was $3,419, or $41,028 annually. If the worker is married, his or her spouse's income would be calculated and assessed separately. A joint family income of a married couple over $60,000 is considered quite high. Most women work, at least part-time, while 90 percent of men have full-time jobs. When women work full-time, they are paid an average of 92 percent of what men are paid. Income tax on businesses is 28 percent, and generally Sweden is considered "business friendly." Real estate is taxed annually at 1 percent of taxable value, but there is no property tax on newly built homes for the first five years, and for the next five years property is taxed at half the normal rate.

Two very sharp differences between the United States and Sweden in the realm of taxation are a national "wealth tax" and a national "value-added" tax or sales tax.

The average family in Sweden is neither rich nor poor but has net assets of approximately $41,000, mostly tied up in housing. For wealthier married couples (by Swedish standards) with assets over $260,000, there is assessed annually a wealth tax of 1.5 percent. The United States has no similar tax on accumulated wealth.

The value-added sales tax is far more regressive because it applies uniformly to all purchases of good and services regardless of wealth, but is similar to many other European Union countries. The rate is a whopping 25 percent on all purchases except food, which is 12 percent, and books and daily newspapers (6 percent). To put these high consumption taxes in context, remember that a visit to the family doctor is $15 (children's visits are free) and the daily fee in the hospital is $10.50; college tuition is free. A serious illness in the family or the cost of higher education doesn't destroy a family's savings.

Both taxes and public services are high in Sweden compared to other countries. When you compare Sweden to the United States, individual Swedes pay less for their military establishment, their health care, and higher education than individual Americans must pay. The cost of paying interest on the national debt is minuscule in Sweden, whereas interest on America's national debt, which is borne by all citizens, is growing larger and more burdensome each year.

In summary, taxes in Sweden, when compared to the United States, are relatively low on businesses; higher on individual income; low on property taxes; very high on consumption; and modest on accumulated wealth (the United States has no wealth tax). Sweden has no overall estate tax similar to the United States. But it does levy an inheritance tax on property received through inheritance that varies depending upon the relationship to the deceased.

CHAPTER 18

Foreign Policy:
War or Peace

A S I HAVE SAID BEFORE, Sweden and the United States are very similar, but have a few obvious differences such as land area and population. Both are highly industrialized Western democracies with free market economies that generate substantial national wealth for their respective nations. However, when we compare the foreign policies of the two countries, what a difference!

Since 1950 the United States has become the dominant military power on the planet and has fought the Korean War, the Vietnam War, the cold war, and two Iraq wars. Consistent with the new Bush Doctrine of "preemptive war" "or war of choice," it even invaded Iraq, a country that posed no imminent threat to its neighbors or to America, and had no connection to the 9/11 World Trade Center attack. Since 2000, the government has increasingly acted unilaterally in foreign affairs. The Vietnam War in the '60s and '70s and the current war in Iraq have divided the country over the wisdom and morality of foreign wars.

During this same time period Sweden's principal foreign policy aim has been to avoid all wars. This has been almost universally supported by its populace. Its foreign policy has been and remains today characterized as neutrality in war and nonalignment in peace, while maintaining a strong home defense. In addition, it has remained active and supportive in multilateral organizations such as the United Nations, the Nordic Council, and the European Union.

In past centuries, Sweden was constantly at war, but these adventures in combat and imperialism lost their attraction long ago. With a conviction that military conflict is always destructive and expensive and with an unswerving dedication to neutrality, together with some good luck, it has avoided war for two hundred years. Swedes have been active in the United Nations, which their country joined from its inception in 1946. One of the first UN secretaries-general was Dag Hammarskjöld, whose father had been the prime minister of Sweden. He brought prominence to the newly formed UN and his devotion to the concept of nations large and small working together to ensure world peace helped keep many members actively involved, even when some questioned the validity of the whole organization. He served as secretary-general from 1953 to 1961, when he died in an airplane crash while on a peacekeeping mission to the Congo. He was posthumously awarded the Nobel Peace Prize.

Other well-known Swedes who have accepted assignments from the United Nations are Carl Bildt, a former prime minister, who served as a peace negotiator in the Balkans in the 1990s; Hans Blix, the head arms inspector before the current war in Iraq; and Folke Bernadotte, a nephew of the Swedish king, who was murdered while on a UN peace mission to the Middle East in 1948.

Many who know Sweden's reputation as a peace-loving country are surprised to learn that it spends 2 percent of its GDP on its defense budget and for years has had a compulsory military service system. This interest in a strong defense comes from the legacy of World War II and Sweden's close proximity to Soviet Russia and Nazi Germany. For years, Swedes have been living in a very dangerous neighborhood. During the cold war, Denmark and Norway opted for membership in the North Atlantic Treaty Organization, but Sweden declined because of NATO's military nature. Instead, it followed a public policy of nonalignment in peacetime in the hope this would allow it to be neutral in case of war. At the same time, Swedes worked to reduce East-West tensions while bolstering their own defense.

The army, navy, and air force have a permanent professional core that is enhanced by recruits from the compulsory service that are inducted and trained each year. The length of training depends on the branch of service and the specialization. At age eighteen, all men are called by conscription to determine if they are fit for military service. Women are not drafted but may join in the officer corps of all three branches if they're tested and found qualified. At age twenty, Swedish men are actually inducted and spend between seven and fifteen months doing basic training. From then on, until age forty-seven, they are regularly called back for military refresher courses. Conscientious objection is an option, and for these men alternative service assignments are given. This system gives the country about 180,000 men easily and quickly mobilized, plus about 70,000 in the so-called Home Guard.

In order to increase the credibility of the country's nonalignment policy, military equipment has been designed and built domestically whenever possible. Because Sweden already had excellent design and manufacturing capability, this was done so successfully that the armaments industry has become an important contributor to the national economy and Sweden has become an active participant in the global weapons market. The Swedish company Bofors Defence has manufactured and sold armaments since World War I.

Where does that leave Sweden in relation to atomic weapons? Today the country has none and supports the abolition, if not the strict worldwide restriction, of all weapons of mass destruction. For a short time in the early 1960s, the Swedish military, government, and public supported the development of a number of small atomic bombs to be used defensively to strike at any invading force. When the project began, there were relatively few atomic weapons in the world beyond the United States' and Russia's, but that didn't last long as the cold war escalated. The expansion of the United States' and Russia's nuclear arsenals, and the development of intercontinental ballistic missiles (ICBMs) and hydrogen bombs, left Sweden and the other Nordic countries caught in the middle and changed the situation completely. To build a few atomic bombs to fend off the Soviet Union would be a possible invitation to annihilation. Rationality prevailed, and in 1968 the government announced a halt to its atomic program and joined the group of sixty-two nations that signed the Treaty on the Non-Proliferation of Nuclear Weapons the same year. Since that time, close to forty years, Sweden has worked closely with its neighbors to keep nuclear weapons out of the region.

During the cold war era, it is understandable that Sweden felt the need to maintain a strong defensive posture. But in recent years the fear of an expansionist Russia and an aggressive Germany has subsided (this is certainly true in the case of Germany), so criticism of the need for an expensive military establishment has grown. However, abolition of some compulsory military training or optional service is unlikely because it is considered a shared unifying experience for all young Swedish men. This situation will undoubtedly play itself out through the democratic process in coming years. Like taxpayers in all countries, Swedes are concerned about wasting public money that could be used on higher priorities, but there are always debates over what these "higher priorities" are.

Before comparing America's foreign policy with Sweden's, a clarifying point should be made about the meaning of the words "defending the country" and "fighting for freedom." To Swedes, these notions refer to the immediate defense of their borders. In the United States, these words have been given a more expansive meaning by our military and political leaders and have led to divisive misunderstandings and widespread national skepticism.

The United States, of course, has much more money than Sweden and that fact has allowed it to build a much more expensive military establishment. During the cold war's arms race, when the Soviet Union and the United States were competing to see which country could stockpile the most atomic bombs and ICMBs, we developed not just hundreds but thousands of atomic warheads.

Today the United States spends more on "defense" than the next fifteen to twenty biggest spenders combined! It amounts to 20 percent of the federal budget. It has overwhelming nuclear superiority, with Russia running a poor second. The only problem is how these stockpiles of atomic weapons can be safety reduced, not increased. (When other countries like Iran or North Korea show any interest in obtaining a few nuclear bombs, all members of the existing "nuclear club," especially the United States, get very nervous.)

In addition to being the number one nuclear power, the United States has the world's dominant air force and the largest navy, with twelve mammoth aircraft carriers that can project power around the globe. It has the most advanced communications and information technology, which demonstrated in Bosnia, Afghanistan, and Iraq that it can destroy targets from the air with remarkable precision. No country in modern history has come close to this overwhelming military dominance and done it after spending less than 5 percent of its GDP. As historian Paul Kennedy notes, "Being Number One at great cost is one thing; being the world's single superpower on the cheap is astonishing."

Other countries are not foolishly attempting to catch up with and challenge America's military superiority, but nevertheless the United States continues to spend more on military research and development than the next six powers *combined*. There is something wrong with this picture.

We are living in a unique time. Wars between nations using both conventional and unconventional weapons are fast becoming obsolete. Organized violence hasn't disappeared, but it is being carried on less by nation against nation and more by relatively small groups of extremists striking out against their own governments or other societies. They are usually called terrorists or sometimes rebels or insurgents. The possibility of traditional military combat between nations is quickly disappearing while the need for homeland security is increasing. It will take time for countries to make the transition. Meanwhile, Sweden maintains a strong defense against foreign invasion and the United States spends billions of dollars on a military that can fight conventional wars on two fronts simultaneously. Additional billions are spent developing a missile air defense system that may never work.

To precisely describe the Untied States' current foreign policy is impossible for me because it has so many contradictory and unformed components. There is, of course, an element of imperialism and hegemony that started with the expansion of the nation soon after it was created and grew through conflicts with Mexico in the 1840s and the Spanish-American War in 1898, which resulted in the acquisition of Puerto Rico and the Philippines. But there has always been something missing in U.S. imperialism. The country has lacked the determination and enthusiasm to occupy and dominate. It came marching home after victories in World War I and World War II and immediately started to disarm. From the beginning it heeded Washington's admonition to avoid "entangling alliances," yet it continues to be driven by a visionary impulse, articulated by Woodrow Wilson, to "make the world safe for democracy." This near-religious impulse can be detected in a nation ready to spend blood and treasure in the Vietnam War and fight the cold war to stop the spread of "atheistic communism" around the world. A grandiose vision to spread democracy and bring peace to the Middle East became the rationale for the invasion of Iraq after the first reason given—finding and destroying weapons of mass destruction—evaporated.

Maybe I could say that the United States' foreign policy is to use its power to shape the world into a collection of true democracies with free markets and exercising free trade so that all can live in peace and prosperity. And, oh yes, to destroy evildoers. We know that wherever the "next" war may take place, in Asia or the Middle East, we will be told that we are "defending" our country and spreading freedom and democracy beyond our shores.

How much the United States will seek allies, and particularly the United Nations, in pursuing its foreign policy aims cannot be accurately predicted. At the present writing, President Bush is seeking all the help he can get from the United Nations in extracting U.S. troops from Iraq. But this is the same President Bush who, in his State of the Union Address in 2004, vowed to Congress and the nation, in an undisguised reference to the United Nations, "America will never seek a permission slip to defend the security of our country" (the statement was received with standing applause). Unfortunately, there is no proof that we needed to invade Iraq to defend our security from any immediate threat.

What is the present foreign policy of the United States, and where is it headed? Unilateralism or multilateralism? Defending threats against the nation through intelligence and homeland security or through wars of choice? World leadership or world domination? I don't know how these questions will be answered.

CHAPTER 19

Why Sweden Works
for Everyone

THIS BOOK HAS ATTEMPTED to explore why Sweden works for everyone. The system Swedes have democratically adopted since 1950 comes from their early roots and is consistent with their Nordic heritage of independence, pragmatism, and striving, mixed with a belief in social justice and the tangible benefits of collective sharing and seeking the common good. Because it has evolved and been criticized, tested and accepted over three generations, it is unlikely to change dramatically anytime soon.

Many elements combine to allow Sweden to work for everyone. For me, the nine most obvious ones are as follows:

- No wars for two hundred years
- No persistent underclass
- Consensus democracy with high voter participation
- Well-educated electorate
- Strong role of women in government and society
- Efficient market economy
- Strong labor unions
- Healthy citizen participation in sports, recreation, and the arts
- Adequately funded public services through taxation

No Wars for Two Hundred Years

One big reason Sweden works for everyone is that there have been no wars for two centuries. Its foreign policy has been non-alignment in peacetime and neutrality in wartime. By maintaining a strong home defense and with some tightrope diplomacy, Sweden had the good fortune to avoid involvement in both World War I and World War II. The people have solidly supported this foreign policy, and, therefore, serious divisions like those experienced in the United States during the Vietnam War and the recent war in Iraq have been avoided. In addition, there has been no growing drain on the country's wealth in order to maintain increasing military expenditures and no ambitious plans to maintain "supremacy" over any other countries.

No Persistent Underclass

In earlier times, Sweden was a class-ridden society with privileges imbedded in custom and law. This is no longer true. All legal distinctions between citizens based on class, gender, sexual orientation, race, and religion have been abolished. Slavery once existed but was abolished in the fourteenth century. Women received complete suffrage in 1920, at the same time this happened in the United States. The small group of Lapps who have lived for centuries in the northern polar regions of Sweden, Norway, and Finland have never been a dependent underclass.

Admittedly, Sweden has long been an ethnically homogeneous society, and only in the twentieth century has there been a significant number of immigrants from countries beyond the Nordic region. Because all citizens are entitled to similar educational, health, and economic benefits, no persistent underclass caused by poverty has developed.

Consensus Democracy with High Voter Participation

Sweden is a democracy in which people participate and vote. In the national election in 2002, 82 percent of eligible voters cast their ballots in Sweden, whereas 51 percent voted in the 2000 U.S. presidential election. (Only 38 percent of eligible U.S. voters living under the poverty line voted.)

In Sweden, the national election, which is held every four years, focuses more on the programs and records of the various political parties running for parliamentary seats rather than on two presidential candidates and their TV appearances and personal style. In other words, citizens vote for a political party and its program, not directly for the prime minister. But, of course, voters know who will become prime minister if that party wins a majority or large plurality of the seats.

The quadrennial national campaigns are mercifully much shorter than those in the United States and turn on issues of substance that affect the future of the nation rather than on quasi-religious "wedge" issues. The effect of money in politics is minimized because campaigns are free of expensive television and radio advertisements. This approach is based on the belief that political ads actually reduce the quality of public discourse, given their usual superficial and negative character. Free time on television is offered to party leaders to answer questions and to debate during the final few weeks of a campaign.

In Sweden, there no longer is a question of whether there should be universal health care, child care, education, and old age pensions provided by or subsidized by the government.

Well-Educated Electorate

Sweden works well as a democracy and a prosperous industrial country because it has had compulsory free universal education since 1842, a policy that has produced literate and well-informed citizens. There is basic nine-year elementary schooling followed by three years of secondary schooling offering seventeen different programs. Every student learns at least one foreign language, beginning in the third grade with English instruction. In the seventh grade, an additional language can be added. In the 1990s, Parliament enacted reforms aimed at curriculum uniformity, gender equality, minority programs, and vouchers for private schools.

For advanced learning, there are now ten universities, plus about twenty smaller public university colleges, eight specialty colleges, and four technical colleges distributed across the country. Tuition is free and students can obtain loans on very good terms for housing and other expenses.

Another option for advanced learning includes traditional "folk schools," which are a type of boarding school in which adults can take a variety of courses, and those who did not finish high school can make up missed courses. The "folk schools" are also frequently used to teach Swedish and other skills to immigrants who have been granted asylum in Sweden.

Nearly one-third of all adults in Sweden take part in some form of adult education. In the evenings, particularly in the winter, regular school buildings are used for adult classes.

Strong Role of Women in Government and Society

Another reason why I think Sweden works well for everyone is that women have a strong voice in government and setting public policy. There are no quotas or token positions set aside for women in government. Through parliamentary elections, 45 percent of the seats are currently held by women, the highest percentage in the world. Until her tragic death in 2003, Anna Lindh, the foreign minister, was considered a favorite to become the next prime minister.

Gender equality has progressed further in many sectors of

Swedish society than perhaps in any other country. One principle of Swedish national policy is that all workers, regardless of gender, should be able to live on their wages or salary and thus not be dependent on others. Sweden has the world's most generous parental insurance system, which enables parents to be at home with their children on paid leave for sixteen months alternating between mother and father.

Internationally, Sweden ranks fourth in the number of women in management, third in the number in government, and first in a UN category called "gender empowerment." Although Sweden has one of the highest rates of women in the workforce (79 percent) and half of the cabinet is female, top business management and corporate boards are heavily dominated by men. This imbalance was a big factor in the recent launch of Sweden's first feminist political party.

Efficient Market Economy

Sweden works for everyone because it has a truly efficient market economy with a tradition of honesty, inventiveness, and entrepreneurship. There is a lack of corporate cronyism whereby CEOs are paid four hundred times what workers receive, and there is no culture of speculation and mismanagement that robs stockholders and devastates workers' jobs and pensions.

An American intellectual property lawyer who has lived and practiced in both countries recently was quoted as saying that in Sweden, "You can depend on business relationships and, when problems come up, you can depend on the [Swedish] courts for fair decisions. That doesn't exist in southern or even central Europe, necessarily, and I've worked enough in New York, New Jersey and Pennsylvania, to know it isn't there either."

A *Business Week* reader who moved from Sweden wrote: "I left Sweden in 1980 because I found it too socialistic. I believed the

U.S. was the right place for my family and business. I have experienced both nations' social policy and see advantages and disadvantages in both. I love America but still I love and understand Sweden. . . . If you move to Sweden, your chances of becoming a billionaire are small, but that is not why people live there. People who want to work and live in Sweden have to accept the values and the ways of life the Swedish system offers. . . . You don't need to earn a lot to live a decent life. Competition is tougher because the home market is smaller and the government has little patience with 'smart' people cheating others with falsified or substandard goods, foods, and services. A bad doctor or lawyer cannot escape the consequences of malpractice."

Strong Labor Unions

One of the continuing strong forces that shapes Sweden's egalitarian society are its labor unions. Currently, an unusually high 80 percent of all employees, private and public, belong to trade unions, including those formed by professional white-collar workers. In the United States in the 1950s, 40 percent of American workers belonged to unions. By 2001, that had dropped to approximately 14 percent. There is no statutory minimum wage in Sweden because with strong unions, collective bargaining agreements have served the same purpose as minimum wage and other work regulations. Until 1970, existing labor laws were few and seldom changed. Since then, there has been legislation more specifically enumerating workers' rights.

The Vocation Act of 1978 increased the statutory minimum paid vacation from four to five weeks. The 1980 Act of Equality Between Men and Women at Work forbids discrimination based on gender. There also must be equal opportunities for employment, on-the-job training, and equal pay for work of equal value.

The Social Democratic Party which presently is the largest

political party, is not formally connected to any labor union but maintains a close informal relationship with the labor movement and is sympathetic and supportive of workers' rights and benefits. The labor unions and the Social Democrats in Sweden have underwritten the nation's large middle class and minimized the gap between rich and poor.

Healthy Citizen Participation in Sports, Recreation, and the Arts

Sweden works for everyone because it has healthy citizens who enjoy an active lifestyle and have an average life expectancy of seventy-seven for men and eighty-two for women, the highest in the world.

When not working or in school, Swedes love to be outdoors. Families hike and camp together, using the thousands of miles of trails that exist in the mountains and forests.

Sweden is a nation of athletes, and more than half the population belong to at least one community sports association or company sports club. The oldest sport is skiing, with downhill slopes and ski jumps scattered throughout the country. Thousands of Swedes participate in cross-country ski races each winter, and hockey is also a popular winter sport.

Both men's and women's soccer teams play in regional international competition. Since the modern Olympic Games started in 1896, Sweden has won more than five hundred medals, including more than two hundred gold medals—a good record for such a tiny nation. There are no professional football, baseball, or basketball leagues similar to those in the United States, and professional boxing is outlawed.

Tennis, also popular in Sweden, has produced such stars as Björn Borg, Stefan Edberg, and Mats Wilander. Between them, Borg and Edberg have won seven Wimbledon Tennis Championships.

Presently, Annika Sörenstam is considered the world's best woman golfer and was named Woman Athlete of the Year by the Associated Press in 2005. Sports are considered an important part of a healthy lifestyle, and girls are encouraged to participate as much as boys.

Most Swedes have four or five weeks of paid vacation, and during the summer, when the sunshine is abundant, they use the time to enjoy the outdoors almost continuously. Water sports are popular, as families take to the country's many thousands of lakes to swim, canoe, and sail.

For many residents of Stockholm, an archipelago of islands stretch nearly ninety miles along the coastline and provides countless recreational opportunities. More than 50,000 homes have been built on the islands and along the shores of the archipelago. Nearly all of these are summer cottages, although 10,000 people have permanent homes there.

Sweden is almost universally literate and enjoys a rich cultural life. To make the arts and cultural events accessible to everyone, the government supports public libraries, cultural magazines, museums, and theaters, as well as dance, music, visual arts, and literature organizations. There was a time when only the aristocracy could enjoy the theater and fine arts, but now art is part of everyday Swedish life. A good example can be found in Stockholm's subway system. Dubbed the world's longest art gallery, more than half of the ninety-nine station stops are decorated with sculptures, engravings, mosaics, and paintings by more than seventy Swedish artists.

Adequately Funded Public Services through Taxation

Swedes aren't in love with high taxes, but they are content with the society taxation makes possible. In Sweden, you get what you pay for. Taxes support excellent education and health care; pen-

sions and child care; military defense and roads and transportation; clean cities with low crime; a clean environment; good jobs
and housing; low national debt; and a social safety net.

Sweden works because its economy works and public services
are supported by sufficient taxes. It also works because there is
constant review and improvement to maintain an efficient productive economy and a happy egalitarian society.

In a recent letter to the editor of the *New York Times,* Peter
Hook of New York, accurately contrasted the Swedish system to
that of the United States.

> To the Editor:
> The compensation Goldman Sachs gives to its em-
> ployees at the end of the year is a turnoff, any way you
> look at it. Henry Blodget argues that such a bonanza is
> provided by the unrestrained capitalism that prevails in
> this country, which he promotes as the best economic
> system on the planet.
>
> I am from Sweden, a prosperous, pluralistic country
> where socialism and capitalism walk hand in hand, and
> where a liberal welfare system prevents unfortunate indi-
> viduals from falling deep into poverty and hardship, while
> allowing talented and ambitious individuals to make
> themselves a fortune. Sweden consistently ranks among
> the top three countries in the world whether judged by
> level of democracy or economical competitiveness.
>
> I think individuals and society as a whole are far bet-
> ter off with an economic system that does not have a huge
> polarity in wealth, such as between the homeless person
> and the Goldman employee on Broad Street.
>
> Dec. 21, 2006

Conclusion

A FTER REVIEWING MY MANUSCRIPT before preparing this final chapter, I realized that I should openly confess my deep love for both Sweden and the United States. I now realize more than ever what prompted me to write this book. Any claim that I am writing with detached objectivity would be disingenuous. Further, I don't claim that Sweden is an authentic facsimile for understanding the European Union or all the so-called welfare states of Western Europe. Much has been written about Europe vis-à-vis the United States. Two good recent books are *The United States of Europe* by T. R. Reid (2004) and *The European Dream* by Jeremy Rifkin (2004). My attempt to compare only one country, Sweden, with the United States is obviously less sweeping. A different option to follow would be to attempt a comparison between all Nordic countries and the United States. This approach would paint a similar picture. I selected Sweden alone because of my personal history and also because Sweden is the largest of the Scandinavian countries, both in area and population, with an industrial economy very similar to that of the United States, allowing contrasts to be more easily discussed.

Most of the U.S. media love to lump together all Western European countries as welfare states where growth is stifled by overly generous public benefits. The fact is that each country is unique, and Sweden is one of those European countries with generous public benefits where growth has not been stifled. Its GDP for

2006 was a healthy 4.4 percent while the GDP for the euro-area was much lower at 2.6 percent. The GDP for the United States was 3.3 percent.

Although Swedish and American societies have grown more and more alike over recent decades, very substantial differences in foreign affairs remain. During the 1970s, the Swedish prime minister, Olof Palme reflected popular opinion in his strident criticism of the Vietnam War. Today, the invasion and occupation of Iraq in 2003 have rekindled the Swedish people's almost universal contempt for U.S. foreign policy. It certainly didn't help to have a Swede, Hans Blix, the United Nation's chief arms inspector, treated dismissively by the Bush administration when he reported that there was no evidence of weapons of mass destruction during Bush's run-up to the war. It has made matters worse when it became evident that Blix was right and Bush wrong in starting a war based on "fixed" intelligence, to use the language of the leaked "Downing Street memo."

The Iraq war illustrates the very deep difference between how Sweden and the United States view military power. Swedes clearly feel that the use of military power should be limited to defending a country's borders and contributing to UN peacekeeping missions around the world. Actually, the country has no greater military capability to do more.

The United States, on the other hand, has many other choices. In recent years it hasn't been reluctant to use its military assets well beyond its borders and in different places around the world, such as in Vietnam, Somalia, Panama, Grenada, and Iraq.

During the last century there has existed the continuing impulse to take action to "make the world safe for democracy," to borrow Woodrow Wilson's phrase. Also, President Bush announced in his second inaugural address, in breathtaking rhetoric, "to seek and support the growth of democratic movements and institutions in every nation and culture, with the ultimate goal of ending tyranny in our world."

An almost equal and opposite impulse held by many Americans is the reluctance to interfere militarily in the affairs of other nations because the price in lives and resources is always too high and too unpredictable. This lesson is being learned again in Iraq.

As the Bush administration continues to unravel, it becomes more and more difficult to predict what direction the country will take fiscally and militarily. Sweden's future is easier to predict. It will largely depend on the world economy because it is so heavily dependent on exports. It should remain stable but it may shift somewhat to the right because of the national parliamentary election of 2006. However, there is no reason to expect any sudden dramatic change in public policy. The present government is a coalition of several right-of-center parties led by the Moderate Party. Considering Sweden's history of consensus democracy, no great upheaval can be anticipated.

Sweden is on a much more tranquil path than that of the United States, which is headed for an economic train wreck if deficits continue to remain out of control. All potential solutions like raising taxes and massive cuts in spending, including entitlements and the military, have been met with denial (deficits don't matter) and magical thinking (we'll grow out of deficits) by the Bush administration. The Democrats and the general public have been largely silent.

As the baby boom generation is starting to retire, a vast increase in Medicare and Social Security payments will begin and will be paid presumably by borrowing more and more from foreign banks. Medicare and Medicaid will increase four times faster than Social Security entitlements.

Today the country's current account balance (money owed) as a percentage of GDP is *minus* 6.5 for the United States and *plus* 7.5 for Sweden. That is because Swedes pay taxes to fund what the government spends, while the United States today borrows whatever money the government spends and passes the obligation to future generations.

The United States is faced with some horrendous choices: raise taxes substantially and, in addition, reduce spending substantially for all programs, including the military. The only way this option can be effected in time will be through some honest consensus reached between Republicans and Democrats, who will have to join hands and take the jump together. The time for tactical political advantage is over. The time for painful realism has arrived. The country will not accept a dismantling of Social Security, Medicare, and Medicaid. For openers, universal health care will have to be accepted as a guaranteed right for all citizens. Taxes considered fair will have to be raised, and recent tax cuts for the wealthy will have to be repealed. Military spending will have to be limited to realistic domestic dangers and not extended to visionary adventures in invading and rebuilding other nations. This will require a reversal of thinking that the country can borrow and spend its way out of the fiscal mess it's in. It will take competent, intelligent thinking and planning and enlisting support across party lines and all social groups. The fate of the nation requires it.

Civilisations die from suicide, not by murder.
—ARNOLD TOYNBEE

Select Bibliography

Barone, Michael. *Our Country: The Shaping of America from Roosevelt to Reagan.* New York: Macmillan, 1990.

Beard, Charles and Mary. *A Basic History of the United States.* New York: Doubleday, 1944.

Ehrenreich, Barbara. *Nickel and Dimed: On (Not) Getting By in America.* New York: Henry Holt, 2001.

Gates, William H., Sr., and Chuck Collins. *Wealth and Our Commonwealth: Why America Should Tax Accumulated Fortunes.* Boston: Beacon Press, 2002.

Hacker, Jacob S. *The Great Risk Shift.* New York: Oxford University Press, 2006.

Lindert, Peter H. *Growing Public: Public Spending and Economic Growth since the Eighteenth Century.* Cambridge: Cambridge University Press, 2004.

Micklethwait, John, and Adrian Wooldridge. *The Right Nation: Conservative Power in America.* New York: Penguin, 2004.

Nordstrom, Byron J. *The History of Sweden.* Westport, CT: Greenwood Press, 2002.

Peterson, Peter G. *Running on Empty: How The Democratic and Republican Parties Are Bankrupting Our Future and What Americans Can Do about It.* New York: Farrar, Straus and Giroux, 2004.

Phillips, Kevin. *Wealth and Democracy: A Political History of the American Rich.* New York: Random House, 2002.

Scott, Franklin D. *Sweden: The Nation's History.* Enlarged edition. Carbondale: Southern Illinois University Press, 1988.

Zinn, Howard. *A People's History of the United States.* 20th anniversary edition. New York: HarperCollins, 1999.

Index

To order additional copies of *The Swedish Secret*

Web: www.itascabooks.com

Phone: 1-800-901-3480

Fax: Copy and fill out the form below with credit card information. Fax to 952-920-0541.

Mail: Copy and fill out the form below. Mail with check or credit card information to:

Syren Book Company
5120 Cedar Lake Road
Minneapolis, MN 55416

Order Form

Copies	Title / Author	Price	Totals
	The Swedish Secret / **Earl Gustafson**	$15.95	$
	Subtotal		$
	7% sales tax (MN only)		$
	Shipping and handling, first copy		$ 4.50
	Shipping and handling, ___ add'l copies @$1.00 ea.		$
	TOTAL TO REMIT		$

Payment Information:

__ Check Enclosed __ Visa/MasterCard	
Card number:	Expiration date:
Name on card:	
Billing address:	
City:	State: Zip:
Signature:	Date:

Shipping Information:

__ Same as billing address __ Other (enter below)	
Name:	
Address:	
City:	State: Zip: